Books by David D. Wilson

A Study on the Holy Ghost
A Study on the Three Johns
The Revelation of Jesus Christ
A Study on the Warnings of Jude
A Study on the Two Peters

Order your copy at:

www.ParadiseGospelPress.com

or contact us at

Paradise Gospel Press
P.O. Box 184
Paradise, Texas 76073

A Study
on the
Three Johns

Rev. David D. Wilson

PARADISE GOSPEL PRESS

A STUDY ON THE THREE JOHNS, Wilson, David D.

First Edition

PARADISE GOSPEL PRESS

www.paradisegospelpress.com

ISBN: 978-1-946823-01-4

Table of Contents

1st John

2nd John

3rd John

Bibliography

Answers

1st John

Introduction to 1st John

In this Bible Study of 1st John, it's my hope to bring to light what John and God want us to understand. Some grownups are still looking for that fairy tale world where all their dreams will come true. We must face it: fairy tales are for children. Most of us have given up looking for a world that doesn't exist. We are members of the here and now. We live in the real world, one that's full of deceit, lies and cruelty, and where nothing seems to satisfy. Our playground has turned into a battleground of good and evil, a world where there's no stable playing field. Everywhere you look you see the fakes and phonies, those who promise you the moon and never deliver anything. It's like cotton candy when you look at it, big and fluffy. You think you have a lot of candy, but when you take that first big bite, you find that it dissolves into nothing. That's the way the world does you. Just when you think you've made it, that you've got what you always wanted, it vanishes into nothing.

What people are really looking for is something that's real, something that's lasting, something to truly satisfy the inner desires of their heart. Wealth and fame we know cannot satisfy; just look at the wealthy and the famous crowd. As a whole, they turn to alcohol and drugs seeking something that will fill that emptiness in their inner being or soul. Many of their cravings for that peace only take them deeper into despair, destroying their lives forever. They search everywhere in the things of this world, but they never try the true source of peace, Jesus Christ.

Here's the problem: In the modern church age, we are overrun with fakes and phonies. Who can we believe? Who can we really trust and have faith in? The answer is those who preach and teach the Bible just like it is and live their lives in accordance with the Word. Take no man's word for anything until you compare it to the scripture for truth. The one and only absolute authority is the Bible. By Bible, I mean the original King James Version; in my opinion the King James is the true authority. It's been used for nearly four hundred years; and by its power and authority, millions if not billions of people have been led to Jesus Christ as their Savior. Then, in the early twentieth century, man decided that the Bible wasn't correct and needed to be changed. Now we have over one hundred versions/translations, where parts have been completely left out and parts have been changed to suit man and his god-like ego. It's no wonder that people are at a loss what to truly believe.

This is the same problem that John faced concerning the church. From the very beginning, there arose false teachers who would try to pervert the gospel and lead good, well-meaning people into apostasy. We have the same problem in today's world. We have two main groups who go from door to door trying to lead Christians who are ignorant of the Bible into their apostate religions. They have a form of godliness, but they deny the truth of the Word. Scripture teaches us that from such we must turn away. (**2 Timothy 3:5** – *Having a form of godliness, but denying the power thereof: from such turn away.*)

These followers of Satan conspire to pull down the church of God, to so dilute the power of the Word that the church loses its focus upon Jesus as the only begotten Son of God. There is a group today who teach that there are other ways to go to heaven besides through Jesus Christ. We know this is a lie of the devil, because scripture says so. (**John 10:7-9** – *[7] Then said Jesus unto them again, Verily, verily, I say unto you, I am the door of the sheep. [8] All that ever came before me are thieves and robbers: but the sheep did not hear them. [9] I am the door: by me if any man enter in, he shall be saved, and shall go in and out, and find pasture.* **John 14:6** – *Jesus saith unto him, I am the way, the truth, and the life: no man cometh unto the Father, but by me.* **1 Timothy 2:5** – *For there is one God, and one mediator between God and men, the man Christ Jesus*;) John wants to bring the church's focus, their spiritual minds, back to the truth of the gospel, the truth that Jesus is the Christ and that there is no other way to make heaven their home except through Jesus.

In John's day, there were many false teachers, but there were three that appear to be the worst. *John Phillips Commentary* says: "Three major heresies had made inroads into the church when John wrote toward the end of the first century of the Christian era. The Ebionites denied the deity of Christ – to them He was just another created being. The Docetists denied the humanity of Christ. Believing that He had not come in the flesh, they taught that He was some kind of phantom who had no corporeal being. The Cerinthians denied the union of the two natures of Christ (the human and the divine). Their notion was that "the Christ" descended upon the man, Jesus, at the time of His baptism and departed from Him at the time of His crucifixion. John indignantly denied all three heresies." Satan's efforts to destroy the church is nothing new. From the time the gospel was first preached until now, the battle has been going on. God has always had a remnant that will serve Him. Are you part of that remnant? (**Jeremiah 23:3** – *And I will gather the remnant of my flock out of all countries whither I have driven them, and will bring them again to their folds; and they shall be fruitful and increase.* **Romans 11:5** – *Even so then at this present time also there is a remnant according to the election of grace.*)

As John was concerned about the church in his day and did his best to keep it true to the Lord, it now behooves you and I to take up the cross. It falls to us to carry on where John left off. We are to preach the true Word of God, to open people's eyes to the dangers around them, and to anchor them to the precious cross, in the true Word of God. As John begins to write this epistle, we need to remember that he was a very old man. He knew that his days on earth were numbered, and that what he did, he must do quickly. John's life was a long one and filled with so much that he had heard and seen. He was one of the twelve disciples called by Jesus. In his beginnings, John had lived in Bethsaida, a fishing village. As far as we know he was a member of a family of four: his father, a fisherman; his mother, Salome; himself and his brother James. John was close to the Lord, a member of the inner circle with Peter and James, his brother. John walked with the Lord, was taught by the Lord, saw the miracles and was there when Jesus ascended back into heaven. John had firsthand knowledge of Jesus. As we study 1st John, we will find that John looked at everything in certain terms, either right or wrong, black or white, light or dark, love or hate or life or death. Sin is sin, and there's no such thing as "bad sin" and "not so bad sin." Sin is sin, and sin condemns the soul of man to a devil's hell.

Bro. David D. Wilson

Chapter 1

1 John 1:1

*That which was from the beginning, which we have heard,
which we have seen with our eyes, which we have looked
upon, and our hands have handled, of the Word of life;*

**The book of Saint John starts where all narratives
should start: in the beginning**. Saint John 1:1 tells us: "*In the
beginning was the Word, and the Word was with God, and the
Word was God.*" John is making it plain that **Jesus was there
when the world was created**, that **He was involved in the creation work**, that **Jesus is God** (the Son of God) and **He and His
Father are one**. Some people have a problem with the fact that
Jesus was man and God at the same time. They ask, was He God
or was He man? They don't seem to be able to understand that
Jesus was God in a man's body. If we look at His birth, we see
that Mary was a virgin, that the Holy Ghost moved within her and
she became with child. The child's Father was God. This child,
like all children, was born of His mother's womb. Like all children, He had to learn to crawl before He could walk and run. The

Note: In this study, all scripture is quoted from the *King James Version*
unless otherwise stated. All scriptures are italicized.

difference was in His loving nature, because He knew who He was and what He came to earth to do.

At the age of twelve, He was found in the temple sitting amid the doctors asking questions, and they "were astonished at his understanding and answers." About the age of thirty, He began His ministry with signs and wonders following, then at the end of three-and-a-half years of preaching and healing the sick, Jesus was crucified on a cross for the sins of the whole world. After His death and resurrection, the disciples began to preach the gospel of Jesus Christ; and the church came into being and began to grow and spread.

All of this brings us to the first Epistle of John and why he wrote it. **John was worried about the church, because false teachings were coming in.** These false teachings were leading people away from the truth of God's Word. At this time, John was a very old man, but he felt that he had to do something. So, his only option was to write letters to remind these saints of the importance of staying true to the Word of God and what they had been taught from the beginning, lest there come in those who would lead them away unto falsehoods, teaching the doctrines of men. Satan is a very serious enemy; his goal is to destroy the church of the Living God. One thing we must remember is that **for everything God has, the devil has a counterfeit.** Scripture tells us that there will come in those who have a form of godliness but deny the power thereof and from such to turn away.

2 Timothy 3:5

Having a form of godliness, but denying the power thereof: from such turn away.

This is the message of 1st John. As we look into the scriptures, it is our aim to shed light on John's intent, as he wrote his epistles to the churches.

"That which was from the beginning . . ." In Verse 1, **John wasn't speaking of the creation of the world**, but of Jesus and His life, and His preaching of the gospel to man. God revealed to John about the creation of the world, as John wasn't there. But John was with Jesus. John was one of the first disciples that Jesus called, along with Peter and James. **John was an eyewitness** to the ministry of Jesus; this was something **he knew personally**. John goes into detail about Jesus to falsify the claims of the religious sects that were trying to lead people away from the truth. John gives an eyewitness account because he was there, the Gnostics were not, and their information came from their imagination or what they supposed to be true. John goes on to remind the church that **he had heard the words, the teachings of Jesus with his own ears**. He knew the truth, and there was no guesswork; he was there during it all. **He walked with Jesus and talked with Jesus**. For three-and-one-half years, he was an interactive part of Christ's life and ministry. **He saw the dead raised to life**, and **he saw the blind and deaf made to see and hear**. **He saw the demons cast out** and peace once again come into people's lives, leaving them free from torment. All these things John heard and saw, oh, what memories he must have had, to have walked with the Master. John goes on to say that their hands (the disciples) had handled the Lord; in other words, they had touched Him on many occasions.

As this passage ends, **John calls Jesus the Word of life**; the Creator of this world, the Word, the Son of God. In *The Wiersbe Bible Commentary*, the author makes note of Jesus being called the Word. "Why does Jesus Christ have this name? Because Christ is to us what our words are to others. Our words reveal to others just what we think and how we feel. Christ reveals to us the mind and heart of God. He is the living means of communication between God and men. To know Jesus Christ is to know God.

"John made no mistake in his identification of Jesus Christ. Jesus is the Son of the Father – the Son of God. John warned us several times in his letter not to listen to the false teachers who tell lies about Jesus Christ. If a man is wrong about Jesus Christ, he is wrong about God, because Jesus Christ is the final and complete revelation of God to men."

False teaching was so bad in John's day (just as today), that **John warns the church to not even let them come into their homes**. We have the same problem today, the occult groups going from door to door leading people astray and away from the truth.

1 John 1:2

(For the life was manifested, and we have seen it, and bear witness, and shew unto you that eternal life, which was with the Father, and was manifested unto us;)

John in this second verse reinforces what he said in the first verse. *"For the life was manifested,"* or visible; Jesus the eternal life came in the flesh, so that man might see and hear him proclaim the way for man to share in this eternal life through Him, the Son of God. **At the time John wrote these letters, there were very few people still alive that had seen and heard Jesus in His earthly ministry.** Again, John affirms that he had seen Jesus and heard him teach, that he was there when Jesus preached the sermon on the mountain and that he was there when Jesus turned the water into wine. He was present when Jesus called Lazarus and raised him from the dead. It was there at the tomb where Jesus told everyone, "I am the resurrection, and the life." In the next verse, He said, "And whoseoever liveth and believeth in me shall never die."

John 11:14-44

[14] Then said Jesus unto them plainly, Lazarus is dead.

[15] And I am glad for your sakes that I was not there, to the intent ye may believe; nevertheless let us go unto him.

[16] Then said Thomas, which is called Didymus, unto his fellow disciples, Let us also go, that we may die with him.

[17] Then when Jesus came, he found that he had lain in the grave four days already.

[18] Now Bethany was nigh unto Jerusalem, about fifteen furlongs off:

[19] And many of the Jews came to Martha and Mary, to comfort them concerning their brother.

[20] Then Martha, as soon as she heard that Jesus was coming, went and met him: but Mary sat still in the house.

[21] Then said Martha unto Jesus, Lord, if thou hadst been here, my brother had not died.

[22] But I know, that even now, whatsoever thou wilt ask of God, God will give it thee.

[23] Jesus saith unto her, Thy brother shall rise again.

[24] Martha saith unto him, I know that he shall rise again in the resurrection at the last day.

[25] Jesus said unto her, I am the resurrection, and the life: he that believeth in me, though he were dead, yet shall he

live:

26 And whosoever liveth and believeth in me shall never die. Believest thou this?

27 She saith unto him, Yea, Lord: I believe that thou art the Christ, the Son of God, which should come into the world.

28 And when she had so said, she went her way, and called Mary her sister secretly, saying, The Master is come, and calleth for thee.

29 As soon as she heard that, she arose quickly, and came unto him.

30 Now Jesus was not yet come into the town, but was in that place where Martha met him.

31 The Jews then which were with her in the house, and comforted her, when they saw Mary, that she rose up hastily and went out, followed her, saying, She goeth unto the grave to weep there.

32 Then when Mary was come where Jesus was, and saw him, she fell down at his feet, saying unto him, Lord, if thou hadst been here, my brother had not died.

33 When Jesus therefore saw her weeping, and the Jews also weeping which came with her, he groaned in the spirit, and was troubled,

34 And said, Where have ye laid him? They said unto him, Lord, come and see.

35 Jesus wept.

36 Then said the Jews, Behold how he loved him!

37 And some of them said, Could not this man, which opened the eyes of the blind, have caused that even this man should not have died?

38 Jesus therefore again groaning in himself cometh to the grave. It was a cave, and a stone lay upon it.

39 Jesus said, Take ye away the stone. Martha, the sister of him that was dead, saith unto him, Lord, by this time he stinketh: for he hath been dead four days.

40 Jesus saith unto her, Said I not unto thee, that, if thou wouldest believe, thou shouldest see the glory of God?

41 Then they took away the stone from the place where the dead was laid. And Jesus lifted up his eyes, and said, Father, I thank thee that thou hast heard me.

42 And I knew that thou hearest me always: but because of the people which stand by I said it, that they may believe that thou hast sent me.

43 And when he thus had spoken, he cried with a loud voice, Lazarus, come forth.

44 And he that was dead came forth, bound hand and foot with graveclothes: and his face was bound about with a napkin. Jesus saith unto them, Loose him, and let him go.

John says, I'm a witness; I'm not lying to you. I'm telling you the truth. I'm trying to show you what the Lord did and can do today. He was made flesh for you and me. **The people that John was writing to only knew of the Jesus that they had heard of and that they had experienced at salvation.** John is saying, believe me, believe me, I won't lead you astray. Listen and learn what God has done for you because He loves you so much.

1 Peter 1:8

Whom having not seen, ye love; in whom, though now ye see him not, yet believing, ye rejoice with joy unspeakable and full of glory:

We don't have to see Jesus to believe; we have felt His saving grace and power, and that power has transformed our lives. We've been changed, the old carnal man who desires the things of the world is dead, and in his place is a new man in Christ Jesus, whose desire now is to serve God and live a life that is pleasing unto the Lord. What a difference Jesus makes in our hearts. Jesus called the Pharisees the children of the devil, and they were the religious sect of that time. What Jesus really was saying is that these Pharisees were counterfeits of what they should have been. To quote *The Wiersbe Bible Commentary:* "A counterfeit Christian – and they are common – is something like a counterfeit ten-dollar bill."

Suppose you have a counterfeit bill and think it's genuine. You use it to pay for a tank of gas. The gas station manager uses the bill to buy supplies. The supplier uses the bill to pay the grocer. The grocer bundles the bill up with forty-nine other ten dollar bills and takes it to the bank. And the teller says, I'm sorry, but this bill is counterfeit.

That ten-dollar bill may have done a lot of good while it was in circulation, but when it arrived at the bank, **it was exposed for what it really was** and put out of circulation.

So it will be with a counterfeit Christian. He may do many good things in this life, but when he faces the final judgment, he will be rejected. *"Many will say to me in that day, Lord, Lord, have we not prophesied in thy name? And in thy name have cast out demons? And in thy name done many wonderful works? And then will I profess unto them, I never knew you; depart from me ye that work iniquity."* (Matthew 7:22-23)

Each of us must ask himself honestly, Am I a true child of God, or am I a counterfeit Christian? Have I truly been born of God? If you have never truly met Jesus and made him your personal Savior, **there's no time like the present to invite Him into your heart and life**, to truly know that you know you are saved, born again, blood washed and on your way to heaven as a child of God. As one man once said, "How sweet it is." Truer words have never been spoken. How sweet it is to trust in Jesus, the lover of my soul.

1 John 1:3

That which we have seen and heard declare we unto you, that ye also may have fellowship with us: and truly our fellowship is with the Father, and with his Son Jesus Christ.

This third verse carries the same message as verses one and two. John is so desirous that the church believes what he's saying, that he repeats it over and over. Remember when we were in school, how **we learned our lessons by repeating or writing them over and over** until we knew how to spell our words, or recite a poem for the class? This is what John is doing, trying to instill the message of Jesus Christ within their minds.

Then John begins to talk about fellowship. We need and must have fellowship with our Lord. **This constant fellowship is what helps keep our lives in line with God and his word.** This fellowship comes on a greater level as we study God's Word and pray every day. Keeping in the word and praying form a tight bond which keeps our minds focused on the good things of God.

Timothy 2:15

Study to shew thyself approved unto God, a workman that needeth not to be ashamed, rightly dividing the word of truth.

We must have fellowship with God every day. At the same time, it is very important that Christians have fellowship one with another. What I am speaking about is churches getting together for a worship service, afterwards enjoying a meal or something where Christian brothers and sisters can talk and enjoy each other's company, a time of being with those who are of like faith. **Fellowship must also be practiced among the church family.** We must realize that we are not just families who go to church, but that everyone in the church is part of the family of God. That's why we call each other brother or sister, because we are. We have our immediate family, but as Christians our family is part of a bigger family, our church family, which is part of a bigger family, the family of God. A very wise man said one time that **fellowship is more than one fellow in the same ship**. Without fellowship, we sometimes get to the place where we feel like no one cares but us, that we are all alone. We sometimes feel like Elijah, but, like Elijah we are not alone. There are many pastors who today have that feeling of loneliness. I would encourage these pastors to join a fellowship or even start a fellowship with like-minded churches. **Don't try to make this journey alone.**

1 John 1:4

And these things write we unto you, that your joy may be full.

John is telling the Christians that the reason for his letters to them is to encourage them to enter unto the fellowship with him. This fellowship that we have with the Father and the Son, our connection with Jesus and God, brings a joy into our heart and lives. It's a lasting joy that will remain in the trials of this life. We must remember that there's a difference between joy and happiness. Joy is lasting, and it comes from the heart; happiness or fun is momentary and fades away. We can have fun with our friends, but when they leave, the fun comes to an end. **The joy from serving God lasts as long as we walk with the Master.** The devil makes it his job to try and rob us of that joy and sometimes succeeds. That's when we must do like King David and go before the Lord and ask God to restore the joy of our salvation.

Psalm 51:8-12

> [8] *Make me to hear joy and gladness; that the bones which thou hast broken may rejoice.*
> [9] *Hide thy face from my sins, and blot out all mine iniquities.*
> [10] *Create in me a clean heart, O God; and renew a right spirit within me.*
> [11] *Cast me not away from thy presence; and take not thy holy spirit from me.*
> [12] *Restore unto me the joy of thy salvation; and uphold me with thy free spirit.*

Despite what the world says about Christians, we aren't missing out on anything. **God never asked us to give up anything that He does not replace with something far better.** *The Wiersbe Bible Commentary* states: "Karl Marx wrote, 'The first requisite for people's happiness is the abolition of religion.'" But the apostle John wrote, in effect, "Faith in Jesus Christ gives you a joy that can never be duplicated by the world. I have experienced this joy myself, and I want to share it with you." We came to Jesus because we lacked joy and fulfillment. There was something missing in our lives, and the pleasures of this world could not fill it. **It could only be filled by the love of God.** John testified of the goodness of God and the joy that walking with Christ could give.

1 John 1:5

This then is the message which we have heard of him, and declare unto you, that God is light, and in him is no darkness at all.

John wants the Christian to see what he's speaking of, the message that carries great truth, the message that he heard Jesus expound upon, that **God is light**. I know this is an old example, but it's a good one. Go into a totally dark room, light one candle and watch what happens to the darkness. The light drives the darkness away, but there's no way possible that the darkness can do anything to the light. **Where there's light, there's no darkness.** That's the way God is. God is light, and no darkness can come into his presence. Before we gave our hearts to Jesus and accepted Him as our Savior, our souls were filled with darkness and blackness. But when we invited Jesus to come into our hearts, the light of God drove out all the darkness and caused us to live and walk in the marvelous light of God's love. The world doesn't understand us; it can't because the world walks in the darkness of Satan. **We have given up our citizenship to this world and are now strangers and pilgrims on this earth.** And like Abraham of old, we look for a city whose builder and maker is God, that holy city of God that we are told about in Revelation.

Revelation 21:1-7

¹ And I saw a new heaven and a new earth: for the first heaven and the first earth were passed away; and there was no more sea.

² And I John saw the holy city, new Jerusalem, coming down from God out of heaven, prepared as a bride adorned for her husband.

³ And I heard a great voice out of heaven saying, Behold, the tabernacle of God is with men, and he will dwell with them, and they shall be his people, and God himself shall be with them, and be their God.

⁴ And God shall wipe away all tears from their eyes; and there shall be no more death, neither sorrow, nor crying, neither shall there be any more pain: for the former things are passed away.

⁵ And he that sat upon the throne said, Behold, I make all things new. And he said unto me, Write: for these words are true and faithful.

⁶ And he said unto me, It is done. I am Alpha and Omega, the beginning and the end. I will give unto him that is athirst of the fountain of the water of life freely.

⁷ He that overcometh shall inherit all things; and I will be his God, and he shall be my son.

Revelation 21:9-27

⁹ And there came unto me one of the seven angels which had the seven vials full of the seven last plagues, and talked with me, saying, Come hither, I will shew thee the bride, the Lamb's wife.

¹⁰ And he carried me away in the spirit to a great and high mountain, and shewed me that great city, the holy Jerusalem, descending out of heaven from God,

¹¹ Having the glory of God: and her light was like unto a stone most precious, even like a jasper stone, clear as crystal;

¹² And had a wall great and high, and had twelve gates, and at the gates twelve angels, and names written thereon, which are the names of the twelve tribes of the children of Israel:

¹³ On the east three gates; on the north three gates; on the south three gates; and on the west three gates.

¹⁴ And the wall of the city had twelve foundations, and in them the names of the twelve apostles of the Lamb.

¹⁵ And he that talked with me had a golden reed to measure the city, and the gates thereof, and the wall thereof.

¹⁶ And the city lieth foursquare, and the length is as large as the breadth: and he measured the city with the reed, twelve thousand furlongs. The length and the breadth and the height of it are equal.

¹⁷ And he measured the wall thereof, an hundred and forty and four cubits, according to the measure of a man, that is, of the angel.

¹⁸ And the building of the wall of it was of jasper: and the city was pure gold, like unto clear glass.

¹⁹ And the foundations of the wall of the city were garnished with all manner of precious stones. The first foundation was jasper; the second, sapphire; the third, a chalcedony; the fourth, an emerald;

²⁰ The fifth, sardonyx; the sixth, sardius; the seventh, chrysolite; the eighth, beryl; the ninth, a topaz; the tenth,

a chrysoprasus; the eleventh, a jacinth; the twelfth, an amethyst.

21 And the twelve gates were twelve pearls; every several gate was of one pearl: and the street of the city was pure gold, as it were transparent glass.

22 And I saw no temple therein: for the Lord God Almighty and the Lamb are the temple of it.

23 And the city had no need of the sun, neither of the moon, to shine in it: for the glory of God did lighten it, and the Lamb is the light thereof.

24 And the nations of them which are saved shall walk in the light of it: and the kings of the earth do bring their glory and honour into it.

25 And the gates of it shall not be shut at all by day: for there shall be no night there.

26 And they shall bring the glory and honour of the nations into it.

27 And there shall in no wise enter into it any thing that defileth, neither whatsoever worketh abomination, or maketh a lie: but they which are written in the Lamb's book of life.

How do we stay saved? It's simple, by staying in the light, as He is in the light.

1 John 1:6

If we say that we have fellowship with him, and walk in darkness, we lie, and do not the truth:

All through this book, John is very concerned about the

truth. These epistles were written because of **heresies that had come into the church to destroy and scatter the flock of God**. These people came in just as they do today. They claim to have a new revelation from God. They slowly begin to change the truth of God's Word. They begin to bow at the altar of the world. The world begins to set their moral standards and convictions. **They gain large numbers of followers who think that these false teachers and preachers are great.** So they are in the world's eyes. They have no morals, no conviction, everything is alright and everybody is going to heaven.

But, there's one big problem. **Where do they stand in the eyes of God?** According to the Bible, they are all going to hell together to spend the ages for believing the lies of the devil, because they wouldn't study it out for themselves. There are millions today who claim to be in fellowship with God. But these same people do not have what they profess to have. **Instead of fellowship with God, they walk in the darkness of this world.** They are lying to those around them, and worse, they are lying to themselves. In the Word, we find where there are those who will turn the truth into a lie.

2 Thessalonians 2:11

And for this cause God shall send them strong delusion, that they should believe a lie:

2 Timothy 4:4

And they shall turn away their ears from the truth, and shall be turned unto fables.

Titus 1:14

Not giving heed to Jewish fables, and commandments of men, that turn from the truth.

Church, in these last days be watchful, for the enemy knows that he only has a short time to work. He is fighting, with everything that God allows, to claim our souls. Pray, study and walk in the light because God is light, and if we walk in the light of God, we will not be led astray. This battle is almost over; we can almost see the lights of home. **Don't give up now, for in truth, Jesus is coming for us.**

1 John 1:7

But if we walk in the light, as he is in the light, we have fellowship one with another, and the blood of Jesus Christ his Son cleanseth us from all sin.

It's strange to me that **people have no respect for God**. You ask them if they believe in God, and the answers vary. Some say, "Oh yes, I believe in God." You ask if they go to church, and most will say no. Others say, "No, I don't believe in God. Why should I? He's never done anything for me." Then there are some who say, "I don't know, nobody's ever proved to me that there's a God." Then, there's another group who say, "I believe in God, and no, I don't go to church. I don't believe in religion where you go to church. They have too many rules, you can't do this, you can't do that, and there are places where Christians can't go. I'm spiritual, I worship God in my own way, so I can do what I want when I want and where I want." They have no concept of what it means to walk in the light of God and to have a close fellowship with God. It's so sad that **most people who claim to be Christians have never had a personal experience with Jesus**. John, as we can see, deals in absolutes; it's light or dark, right or wrong in John's eyes. There's no gray area, no mixing of light and dark to form a shadowy area. **You are either in or out**, and there's no mid-point. This is how it should be. There's no such thing as a little white lie; all lies are of the devil, all liars are of the devil and all liars will find themselves in hell.

Revelation 21:8

> *But the fearful, and unbelieving, and the abominable, and murderers, and whoremongers, and sorcerers, and idolaters, and all liars, shall have their part in the lake which burneth with fire and brimstone: which is the second death.*

Water baptism does not save us; many people go down a dry sinner and come up a wet sinner without any change. **Church membership will not save a soul from hell, either.** Except there be a change of heart, there is no salvation. The blood of Christ cleanses us from sin and changes us from the inside to the outside. It changes how we talk, the things we do, the places we go**. If there is no change, there is no salvation.** For scripture tells us that the old man of sin dies, and a new man rises in righteousness unto the Lord. You will find that I repeat this over and over.

Ephesians 4:24

> *And that ye put on the new man, which after God is created in righteousness and true holiness.*

Colossians 3:9-10

> *⁹ Lie not one to another, seeing that ye have put off the old man with his deeds;*
> *¹⁰ And have put on the new man, which is renewed in knowledge after the image of him that created him:*

We are blood-bought and redeemed by the blood of the Lamb, Jesus Christ. *John Phillips Commentary* puts it this way: "That surely has to be one of the most comforting verses in the whole Bible. It is a truth taught from Genesis to Revelation – **blood cleanses sin**. A skeptic challenged a believer; 'How does blood cleanse sin?' he demanded. The Believer replied with a counter question: 'How does water quench thirst?' he asked. The skeptic replied, 'I don't know, but I know that it does.' 'Just so,' said the believer, 'I don't know how blood cleanses sin, but I know that it does – God says so.' " **The blood, the precious blood that washes white as snow, no greater gift could God give to man.** This gift opens up all eternity for those who accept Jesus as their Savior.

1 John 1:8

> *If we say that we have no sin, we deceive ourselves, and*
> *the truth is not in us.*

The one thing that all men have in common is that each and every one of us has sinned. For all have sinned and come short of the glory of God. If there were no sin in our lives, then we would have no need of salvation. **Sin is anything that comes between us and God.** The devil's desire is to get us to sin and follow after fleshly desires or wants. Satan knows that if he can turn our eyes upon the things of this world and get us to lust after these sinful things, that he has a hold upon us. **Lust for the things of this world will take over our minds and hearts**; like drug addicts whose only thought is where and when to get that next shot or pill, the dope consumes their very lives. This is why we need to be careful before God. Not everyone has trouble with drugs, but sin takes many shapes and forms, each affecting our souls. The answer is to go before the Lord and ask for forgiveness.

1 John 1:9

If we confess our sins, he is faithful and just to forgive us our sins, and to cleanse us from all unrighteousness.

John is telling the world how to receive salvation. **We must repent of our sins, invite Jesus into our lives and let Him live in our hearts.** To keep salvation, to keep this gift of God, we must put the things of this world aside, commit ourselves to live a Christ-like life before the world and be an example to the world of what God can do for us. As John so aptly puts it, **we must walk in the light as He is in the light**. As we journey down this road, we will see many who began this race then turned aside from the truth to go after the things of this world. Can a person backslide and lose their soul to the devil? Yes. While most denominations believe in some sort of eternal security, there's no scriptural basis for this belief. **Scripture states that some will depart from the faith**; they will simply turn their back on God and follow after the devil's crowd. Those who believe in eternal security counter that they were never saved; they just acted like they were. Scripture holds that this cannot be true. **To believe what the scripture states concerning backsliders tears down the doctrine of "once you're saved, you're always saved."**

I worked with a man who was a deacon in his church. He believed in eternal security. I asked him if he lied, cheated, stole, committed adultery, and got drunk before he was saved. He replied that he did. I asked him if God forgave him of his sins when he got saved. He again said yes. Then I pointed out he still did the same things: lied, cheated, stole, ran around on his wife, committed adultery and still got drunk. So just what was he saved from? He told me that when he repented and asked for forgiveness, Jesus washed his sins away and sealed his soul unto eternal security; that his soul was set aside, and the things he did now had nothing to do with his salvation. I told him that **if sin condemned his soul to hell before he was saved, and if he still did the same things after he claimed to be saved, those sins still condemned his soul** to a devil's hell. His reply: Not according to what my church believes.

This type of doctrine is destroying souls. Search the Word. Even Jesus said **no man having put his hand to the plow and looking back is fit for the Kingdom of God**.

Luke 9:62

> *And Jesus said unto him, No man, having put his hand to the plough, and looking back, is fit for the kingdom of God.*

We will get into this question of eternal security and backsliding more in the next chapter. If we are saved we are cleansed from all sin, and Jesus speaks to us and says **"go and sin no more."**

1 John 1:10

If we say that we have not sinned, we make him a liar, and his word is not in us.

This verse explains itself. If any man says that he has not sinned, he is a liar and the truth, it is not in him. Again, **all men have sinned**; that's why Jesus came to pay the price for our salvation. **The shed blood of Jesus is the only thing that can wash away our sins**; nothing else will work. And regardless of what man says and tries to teach, Jesus is the only way to enter into heaven. There is no other way. To claim otherwise is a sin in itself. So, we have all sinned; the Word says we have, and the Word is not a lie. God is not a liar. Jesus is not a liar. Man is the liar, and so will it always be, until we all come to the saving knowledge of Jesus Christ. **Jesus saves by his grace that is bestowed upon us through the blood.** Like the song says:

What can wash away my sin?
Nothing but the blood of Jesus;
What can make me whole again?
Nothing but the blood of Jesus.

We have all sinned; that's why we need to be saved. With salvation comes a new life free from the sins of this world. Our testimony then becomes, I was a sinner, but now, I am saved by grace. When we are saved, we are a sinner no longer, because Jesus has come into our heart to live. Scripture says that no man can serve two masters. **We either serve God, or we serve the devil**; we cannot serve them both at the same time. There is no scriptural way that we can be saved and a sinner at the same time.

Introduction and Chapter One – Test Your Knowledge

1. Our playground has turned into

_____

_____

2. What three main groups were trying to destroy the church?

_____

_____

_____

3. Who made up the inner circle?

_____

_____

_____

4. In the beginning was the

_____

5. Why was John worried about the church?

_____

_____

6. For everything that God has, the devil has a

_____

7. Jesus said I am the resurrection and

_____

8. Jesus called the Pharisees the

_____

9. What is important to every Christian?

_____

_____

10. Joy is lasting while happiness and fun are

_____

11. King David prayed for God to restore the joy of

_____

12. Karl Marx wrote: "The first requisite for people's

happiness is the _____

_____ "

13. God is _____

_____

14. Like Abraham, we are looking for a city whose

_____

_____

15. How do we stay saved?

_____

_____

16. Can a person believe in God and still be lost?

_____

17. Is one lie worse than another?

_____

18. Have all men sinned?

_____

19. Can, according to scripture, a person backslide and lose their soul? _____

20. What is our only way to heaven?

_____

_____

Chapter 2

1 John 2:1-2

¹ My little children, these things write I unto you, that ye sin not. And if any man sin, we have an advocate with the Father, Jesus Christ the righteous:
² And he is the propitiation for our sins: and not for ours only, but also for the sins of the whole world.

These two verses are a continuation of the thought in the last three verses in Chapter One. John says that he's writing to admonish the saints not to sin. God exacts a penalty upon the soul that sinneth, for **God is righteousness, and there can be no unrighteousness in His presence.** Sin separates us from God by words or deeds that bring shame and disgrace upon us. All through scripture we are told that sin brings death. Anything that comes between us and God is sin. The Word tells us to walk in the light as He is in the light. Who is He? His name is Jesus. As long as we walk in the light, there can be no sin in our lives. We need to pray continually, "**Lord, more of Thee, I need more of Thee**," and to get more of Him, there has to be less of us. So, when we're praying, "Lord more of Thee and less of me," **be**

prepared to decrease so that Jesus may increase. Oh, what joy there is in giving ourselves to Jesus completely. If we cannot give ourselves completely, then we need to find out why. There can be all kinds of reasons; mostly it has to do with money and a sense of security. There are so many people that are concerned with money and possessions that it's surprising. They don't seem to understand that these things come and go, but Jesus is eternal. **Don't let the devil get you caught up in the present when eternity is staring us in the face.** I know it's easy to get caught up in a desire for things when we've grown up with little to nothing. But it's time to get our ducks in a row and decide what's important to us.

Luke 12:16-21

16 And he spake a parable unto them, saying, The ground of a certain rich man brought forth plentifully:

17 And he thought within himself, saying, What shall I do, because I have no room where to bestow my fruits?

18 And he said, This will I do: I will pull down my barns, and build greater; and there will I bestow all my fruits and my goods.

19 And I will say to my soul, Soul, thou hast much goods laid up for many years; take thine ease, eat, drink, and be merry.

20 But God said unto him, Thou fool, this night thy soul shall be required of thee: then whose shall those things be, which thou hast provided?

21 So is he that layeth up treasure for himself, and is not rich toward God.

**Be careful in these last days, for we know not
when Jesus shall come.**

John continues that if we sin, **we have an advocate with the Father, who is Jesus Christ our Lord**. As we pointed out in Chapter One, the word says IF we sin. The word if is one of the biggest words in the English language in meaning. An old example is that an army came against a walled city. The commander sent a message to the people inside the city, and the message said: "Surrender now, because if we get over these walls, we will burn your city to the ground." The commander of the city sent back this message: "IF you get over these walls." **John isn't saying that you have a license to sin and do whatever you want**; then just go before the Lord, repent and ask for forgiveness; and God will forgive you.

Sadly, some people have the idea that they can live like the devil Monday through Saturday, go to the church on Sunday and ask for forgiveness, and start all over again on Monday. Some people believe that when they got saved, God sealed up their soul and set it aside. They believe they can (and do) live like they want to: They lie, cheat, steal, get drunk, curse, commit adultery and other things believing that everything is all right with them. They believe if they die or Jesus comes back, they will go to heaven. This is what their church teaches, that once they get saved, their soul is separate, and what they do in the body has no connection on the condition of their souls anymore.

We ask ourselves how can people be so misled, but think about this: **Most people never read their Bibles.** They only know what they hear in church, and if their teachers and preachers are telling them incorrectly, they will never know. This **is why it's so important to read and study God's Word,** to know what the Bible says for yourself. You may be surprised what you will learn.

1 John 2:2

And he is the propitiation for our sins: and not for ours only, but also for the sins of the whole world.

Verse 2 begins by John stating that Jesus is the propitiation for our sins. Propitiate means to become favorably inclined, to appease or conciliate, a sacrifice made to appease. **Jesus came to make reconciliation for the sins of all mankind that we might have access to the throne of God.** There's no need for the priesthood any longer, because we, the born-again believers, have become a royal priesthood, a chosen generation. We are kings and priests before God. Jesus has done this for us, that we might have eternal life through Him.

1 Peter 2:9

But ye are a chosen generation, a royal priesthood, an holy nation, a peculiar people; that ye should shew forth the praises of him who hath called you out of darkness into his marvellous light:

Jesus our Lord and Savior is now at the right hand of God. There **He's making intercession for the saints**, and that's us.

Romans 8:34

Who is he that condemneth? It is Christ that died, yea ra-

ther, that is risen again, who is even at the right hand of
God, who also maketh intercession for us.

Our sins condemned us to a devil's hell; the blood of animals could only postpone our punishment. It could not give us the freedom from sin that was needed. **Jesus came and offered Himself as a supreme sacrifice that we might once and for all be free from sin.** Jesus was the propitiation for our sins. He paid the price at Calvary. Not only was He the propitiation for our sins, but now at the right hand of God, He is our intercessor. As saved, born-again believers, the Word tells us not to sin. The Word tells us to be perfect as God in heaven is perfect. **We can and must strive to be perfect in God's sight.** It can be done. One man told me nobody could be perfect; the only perfect man was Jesus. I asked him if he could live one minute without sinning, and he said yes. Then I asked if he could live five minutes without committing a sin, and he said yes. I told him that if he could go five minutes, then he could go an hour, and if one hour, he could go one day, one week, one month, one year. **We live this life one minute at a time**; don't worry about an hour from now, just live for now.

If we should fall, *if* we should sin, we have an advocate, Jesus Christ, the righteous. Don't wallow in self-pity as so many do. **Ask Jesus for forgiveness, get up and go on living this Christian life.** To wallow in self-pity and regret only serves to pull you down and rob you of your victory in Jesus. The devil is made happy when we have ourselves a pity party and blame ourselves for what the devil has caused and done. We can make the devil happy, or we can make him mad by rebuking him in the name of Jesus and telling him that he is not going to rob us of our joy in Christ Jesus; for **we are made overcomers by the word of**

our testimony and the blood of the Lamb.

Revelation 12:10-11

> *[10] And I heard a loud voice saying in heaven, Now is come salvation, and strength, and the kingdom of our God, and the power of his Christ: for the accuser of our brethren is cast down, which accused them before our God day and night.*
> *[11] And they overcame him by the blood of the Lamb, and by the word of their testimony; and they loved not their lives unto the death.*

The blood of the Lamb, the blood that covers a multitude of sins, the blood that has set us free, **thank God for the blood of Jesus**.

1 John 2:3

And hereby we do know that we know him, if we keep his commandments.

In this third verse, John is giving a formula by which we can judge ourselves. If we know Jesus, that is if we have had a personal experience with Him, then we are going to keep his commandments. This test is given to us by John so that we may judge ourselves in the light of God's Word. Jesus said, *Why call ye me Lord, Lord and do not what I say.*

Luke 6:46-49

⁴⁶ And why call ye me, Lord, Lord, and do not the things which I say?

⁴⁷ Whosoever cometh to me, and heareth my sayings, and doeth them, I will shew you to whom he is like:

⁴⁸ He is like a man which built an house, and digged deep, and laid the foundation on a rock: and when the flood arose, the stream beat vehemently upon that house, and could not shake it: for it was founded upon a rock.

⁴⁹ But he that heareth, and doeth not, is like a man that without a foundation built an house upon the earth; against which the stream did beat vehemently, and immediately it fell; and the ruin of that house was great.

Jesus, in Luke, is saying that **there's no need to call Him Lord, if we're not going to do what He tells us to do**. As we look around us, we see many people who call Jesus Lord, but their lives aren't lived for Jesus. There are many who profess to be Christians but do not possess what they claim to have. When the rapture of the church takes place, a lot of people will be surprised when they are left here. One man said he didn't have to live so strict a life, because Jesus knows we're going to sin every day. So, lighten up. My answer is this: If he's right, then I have nothing to worry about, but if I'm right and he's wrong, then he just missed the rapture. **We are supposed to walk just as close to Jesus as is possible**, but there are great numbers who try to walk just as close to the world as they can and still remain a Christian; this is why so many fall and fail the Lord.

The key to serving God is to stay as far away from the world as possible. **We are in the world, but we are not of the world**, because of salvation. Listen to a lot of people who claim to be Christians, and they tell stories of all the fun, all the pleasure that they had in the world, and they call them the good old days. Often, when people begin to miss the old life, it isn't long before they backslide, and their latter end is worse than their beginning.

2 Peter 2:20-22

> *20 For if after they have escaped the pollutions of the world through the knowledge of the Lord and Saviour Jesus Christ, they are again entangled therein, and overcome, the latter end is worse with them than the beginning.*
> *21 For it had been better for them not to have known the way of righteousness, than, after they have known it, to turn from the holy commandment delivered unto them.*
> *22 But it is happened unto them according to the true proverb, The dog is turned to his own vomit again; and the sow that was washed to her wallowing in the mire.*

The whole key to serving the Lord is to keep His commandments. As we keep His commandments, our lives fill with joy, peace and love. However, we must keep them every day, not just when we feel like it, or when it suits our fancy. I firmly believe that some people get up in the morning and say they don't feel like being a Christian today, so they go about doing their own thing. Then they wonder why God doesn't bless them like He does others. **Why should we expect God to bless us when we don't bless God by living for Him?** God inhabits the praises of His people.

Psalm 22:3

> *But thou art holy, O thou that inhabitest the praises of Israel.*

If we don't give God a life of love and service and praise, then we don't deserve a blessing. Look at all Jesus has done for us, and then ask what we've done for him. I talked to a man the other day; he told me that when he was a young man, he got out of church. He said he raised his kids out of church, and now that he's back in church, he doesn't know how to get his kids in church. This problem is all too common today. I told this man that all he could do was to pray for them and ask God to bring them in. Then talk to them about the Lord and trust God to do the work. **Oh, the mistakes we make when we do our own thing.**

1 John 2:4

He that saith, I know him, and keepeth not his commandments, is a liar, and the truth is not in him.

John is trying to get people to check their lives to be sure where they stand with God. In Verse 3, he tells everyone **a sure way to know if someone loves Christ is if they keep His commandments**. In this verse, he is telling everyone that if they say they love Jesus, and don't keep His commandments, then they are liars, and the truth is not in them. Just like Verse 3, **the true test as to whether you are a Christian or not is whether you keep Jesus' commandments**. It's just that simple.

1 John 2:5

But whoso keepeth his word, in him verily is the love of God perfected: hereby know we that we are in him.

This fifth verse is a continuation of verses three and four.

To the one who keeps the words of Jesus, in them is the true love of God made manifest or perfected. By living our lives according to the words and teachings of Jesus, we perfect ourselves before God. **If our desire is to live for Jesus, to walk according to His commandments; then we know that we can live a perfect life in the sight of God.** People say that it cannot be done, but God's Word says that it can.

Genesis 6:9

> *These are the generations of Noah: Noah was a just man and perfect in his generations, and Noah walked with God.*

Job 1:1, 8

> *[1] There was a man in the land of Uz, whose name was Job; and that man was perfect and upright, and one that feared God, and eschewed evil.*
> *[8] And the LORD said unto Satan, Hast thou considered my servant Job, that there is none like him in the earth, a perfect and an upright man, one that feareth God, and escheweth evil?*

Job 2:3

> *And the LORD said unto Satan, Hast thou considered my servant Job, that there is none like him in the earth, a perfect and an upright man, one that feareth God, and escheweth evil? and still he holdeth fast his integrity, although thou movedst me against him, to destroy him without cause.*

Genesis 5:24

And Enoch walked with God: and he was not; for God took him.

1 John 2:6

He that saith he abideth in him ought himself also so to walk, even as he walked.

This verse goes along with the other three verses, and John is still on the same theme. If a man states that he is saved, then it is his duty to put forth a Christ-like example before this lost and dying world. The world is tired of fakes and phonies; it's looking for the real thing. **If you say you're a Christian, then you had better have the goods**; because the world is going to be watching you, to try and tear you apart. They know who has the power with God and who is pretending. If you claim it, you had better possess it. It's time to stop putting on the show and to put forth the real light of God's love and grace.

1 John 2:7

Brethren, I write no new commandment unto you, but an old commandment which ye had from the beginning. The old commandment is the word which ye have heard from the beginning.

These next five verses are all intertwined, and we'll try to deal with them as a group and singly at the same time. They all deal with Christians loving each other. **Love is a word that ex-**

presses itself in many ways. I love your hat, I love your new coat, I love Mom's cooking. But, Dad, I love this girl; she's everything I want. The word love can be used in so many ways to describe so many things. *The Wiersbe Bible Commentary* states: "Words, like coins can be in circulation for such a long time that they start wearing out. Unfortunately, the word love is losing its value and is being used to cover a multitude of sins. It is really difficult to understand how a man can use the same word to express his love for his wife as he uses to tell how he feels about baked beans! When words are used that carelessly, they really mean little or nothing at all. Like the dollar, they have been devalued."

In 1st John, John deals mainly with three things: love, life, and light; these three describe a Christian's character. We, as Christians, meaning, being Christ-like, **must show the world that Jesus is the answer to the problems of life**. He may not take away our problems. Nevertheless, he gives us the peace that is needed to handle them. True peace is a gift from God, and God desires everyone to have it. The devil can wreak havoc in a person's life if he can take away our God-given peace. How can a person keep that peace? By trusting in God, trusting when it seems like your world is falling apart, trusting when your children aren't living the way you want them to, trusting God to keep your family together, and trusting when it seems that all hope is gone. Jesus tells us to cast all of our cares upon Him, because He cares for us.

1 Peter 5:7

Casting all your care upon him; for he careth for you.

Trust is vital to living this Christian life. **We must trust in Jesus, just as a small child has trust in her parents**, for we are God's children. Above all trust, trust, and again I say trust in the Lord, for trust is faith.

In Verse 7, John says, I am not writing a new commandment unto you, but an old commandment that you have been taught from the very beginning when you first heard the Word of God preached unto you. **God's Word hasn't changed**, though there be some who would pervert the gospel and change the commandments given unto you by the apostles, as spoken by the Lord Jesus Christ. **Christians must express love one for another.** Scripture teaches love. Let's look at what the scripture says:

Leviticus 19:18

Thou shalt not avenge, nor bear any grudge against the children of thy people, but thou shalt love thy neighbour as thyself: I am the LORD.

Deuteronomy 6:5

And thou shalt love the LORD thy God with all thine heart, and with all thy soul, and with all thy might.

Mark 12:28-34

[28] And one of the scribes came, and having heard them reasoning together, and perceiving that he had answered them well, asked him, Which is the first commandment of all?

29 And Jesus answered him, The first of all the commandments is, Hear, O Israel; The Lord our God is one Lord:

30 And thou shalt love the Lord thy God with all thy heart, and with all thy soul, and with all thy mind, and with all thy strength: this is the first commandment.

31 And the second is like, namely this, Thou shalt love thy neighbour as thyself. There is none other commandment greater than these.

32 And the scribe said unto him, Well, Master, thou hast said the truth: for there is one God; and there is none other but he:

33 And to love him with all the heart, and with all the understanding, and with all the soul, and with all the strength, and to love his neighbour as himself, is more than all whole burnt offerings and sacrifices.

34 And when Jesus saw that he answered discreetly, he said unto him, Thou art not far from the kingdom of God. And no man after that durst ask him any question.

Jesus took these two Old Testament scriptures and combined them, saying that there was no greater commandment than this: **To love one another is the fulfilling of the law.** Love is the key, for without love, it is impossible to please God. John states that **God is love.** I've heard different ones say, "I learned to love a certain person." In Christ, we receive the gift of love for everyone at salvation. **We don't have to learn love, for God is love.** True, we don't have to like how a person acts or lives, but there must be a love for that person's soul in our hearts. **We must, and this is vital, learn to separate sin from the sinner.** God hates the sin but loves the sinner. This we must do, also.

Romans 12:9-10

⁹ Let love be without dissimulation. Abhor that which is evil; cleave to that which is good.
¹⁰ Be kindly affectioned one to another with brotherly love; in honour preferring one another;

1 John 2:8

Again, a new commandment I write unto you, which thing is true in him and in you: because the darkness is past, and the true light now shineth.

John, in this verse, says, *I write unto you a new commandment of things that are true, in Him and you*. John is speaking of the great love that Jesus had for the world and for the lost. Now **that love rests within all born-again believers**. Jesus left His church to carry on the work that He started. Jesus picked twelve men to be His disciples. There were others, but these twelve were singled out, and one of them betrayed Him. These men had the job of carrying on what Jesus started, to birth an infant church and establish a proven ministry that would carry the gospel to the whole world. This is why John stresses that we must love one another, **for without love, the message will never reach the lost world** and lost mankind. We must be like Jesus in love and compassion for the lost, and be like Jesus to forgive those who sin against us. For I am persuaded, that Jesus would have forgiven even Judas, if he would have asked for forgiveness. We know that Jesus is the Son of God. But have we ever stopped to think that one of the greatest things about Jesus was His love? He loved everyone, including the poor, and His compassion for them was great.

He even loved his enemies; He loved those who came to arrest Him. He healed the high priest's servant when Peter cut off his ear. He loved the misguided priest who called for his death. He loved the soldiers who crucified Him on the cross. He prayed for them, saying, "Father, forgive them, for they know not what they do." This love that knows no boundaries, **this love is the reason that we are saved today**. Oh, my God, this love, this precious love that cost heaven the best that it had to give. Jesus brought an old truth to the forefront and renewed it into a new truth that we are to love one another.

John 13:34-35

> [34] *A new commandment I give unto you, That ye love one another; as I have loved you, that ye also love one another.*
> [35] *By this shall all men know that ye are my disciples, if ye have love one to another.*

The light of Jesus now shines in the darkness; men can no longer say, "I didn't know." For now, according to the word, *"the darkness is past, and the true light now shineth."* **People can no longer say they didn't know**; we have access to God's Word, and there is gospel being preached on the radio, TV, and the Internet. All around the world, the message is going out: Prepare, for Jesus is coming back.

1 John 2:9

He that saith he is in the light, and hateth his brother, is in darkness even until now.

In Verse 9, John is again talking about walking in the light. He then says that if we hate our brother, we are in darkness. Is John speaking of the lost world? Yes, but this message is two-fold. He's speaking of the world, but he's also speaking of Christians having love one to another. We must love the souls of the lost, but it's a necessity that **Christians have love toward one another**. When we get saved, we have our sins washed away, and that spirit of jealousy and hatred also must vanish. For if we continue to be jealous or have hatred in our heart, we cannot fulfill the commission that Christ sets for his saints. I agree that it's much easier to talk about how a Christian should love everybody than it is to put it into practice. But we must practice Christian love to the saints. Over and over, people say they just don't like someone because they think they are better than everybody else. We must be careful what we say and where we say it, because we never know who might be listening, or what damage we might do to a person's Christian walk with God.

To have dislike or hatred for a fellow child of God will affect our walk with God. A perfect example is to have someone mad or upset with you, and you have no idea what you said or did, or even when. We cannot live our lives in a bubble, but we can walk softly in the Lord. Hatred brings sin into the lives of believers.

When I was a young man with a young family, we attended a small church where the Lord moved mightily. The church grew rapidly till we were overcrowded. We began to make plans to build a new, larger church. For some reason I didn't understand, the pastor became disgruntled with the church people and began to run them off. I now understand his problem was that he thought he was losing control of the situation, and he decided if he ran people off, he could control things. After some time, because of the verbal abuse from behind the pulpit, we also left the church. It would have been so easy to hate that man, but God knows that **we cannot have hatred in our hearts**. Every time I would see that man, God would tell me to go shake his hand. I didn't want to, but I did because God said to. I would walk up to him in public and stick out my hand. I could tell he didn't want to, but he would shake my hand. You might ask why God would tell me to do that. It was for my own good as well as his. It wasn't long before that spirit of dislike was gone in both of us. Sadly, the church declined to so few attendees that it closed its doors.

I often wonder what that church could have been had one man not gotten out of the will of God. We can say that we walk in the light of God's love, but **if there's hatred in our hearts, we are walking in darkness, not love**. It's not easy to love some people, but we must love them as Christ loves them. This is the only way to serve and please God. Hatred is a sin and leads a person to commit other sins before God. If we cannot forgive those who sin against us, then how can God forgive us?

Mark 11:25-26

> [25] And when ye stand praying, forgive, if ye have ought against any: that your Father also which is in heaven may forgive you your trespasses.
> [26] But if ye do not forgive, neither will your Father which is in heaven forgive your trespasses.

Ephesians 5:32

This is a great mystery: but I speak concerning Christ and the church.

Colossians 3:13-14

[13] Forbearing one another, and forgiving one another, if any man have a quarrel against any: even as Christ forgave you, so also do ye.
[14] And above all these things put on charity, which is the bond of perfectness.

1 John 2:10

He that loveth his brother abideth in the light, and there is none occasion of stumbling in him.

Verse 10 is again talking about walking in the light, or living a life in accordance with our salvation. If we say that we are saved and walking in the path Jesus has laid out for us, and we hate our fellow brother or sister, then we are lying to God and ourselves. To quote from *The Wiersbe Bible Commentary*: "This is one reason why God established the local church, the fellowship of believers. 'You can't be a Christian alone;' a person cannot live a complete and developing Christian life unless he is in fellowship with God's people. The Christian life has two relationships: the vertical (Godward) and the horizontal (man-ward). And what God has joined together, man must not put asunder! And each of these two relationships is to be one of love one for the other." Jesus dealt with this matter in the Sermon on the Mount. A gift on the altar was valueless as long as the worshipper had a dispute to settle with his brother.

Matthew 5:21-24

21 Ye have heard that it was said by them of old time, Thou shalt not kill; and whosoever shall kill shall be in danger of the judgment:

22 But I say unto you, That whosoever is angry with his brother without a cause shall be in danger of the judgment: and whosoever shall say to his brother, Raca, shall be in danger of the council: but whosoever shall say, Thou fool, shall be in danger of hell fire.

23 Therefore if thou bring thy gift to the altar, and there rememberest that thy brother hath ought against thee;

24 Leave there thy gift before the altar, and go thy way; first be reconciled to thy brother, and then come and offer thy gift.

It's easy to be a Christian in words only, but another thing to be a Christian in deeds. We should always be truthful; our yea should be yea, and our nay should always be nay. We don't need to be a person who flip-flops back and forth. Truth and love go hand in hand; you cannot have one without the other. Contrary to popular opinion, **love is not blind**; because as we have read, love is light, the light of our lives. People who have hatred in their lives walk in the blackness of darkness without hope. They need the light of God's love abounding in their souls.

There are many stories or examples of hatred in the pages of God's Word. One is told in the Book of Esther. Haman hated the Jewish people so much that he plotted and schemed to have them all killed. His deception became his downfall, and he was hung on the very gallows that he had built. Hatred is a blinding force that affects the world, and it sadly affects the church people as well.

Christian love should be a very practical part of the Christian's everyday life and should control the way we deal with others. **To love other Christians as God loves us is to be Christlike** in the sight of God. Moreover, it leaves us satisfied with ourselves, which is of great importance to our self-esteem. When a child of God has low self-esteem, when they have poor self-worth, it's hard for them to freely love those around them. God's Word tells us to be loving individuals. Nevertheless, it's impossible to truly love others when you don't love yourself. When you look at yourself in the mirror every morning, you need to say, "Gee, you're a good-looking person; I love you like Jesus loves me." You may think this is funny, but when a person is told that they look good, it lifts their spirits all day long.

Husbands, tell your wives that you love them. It won't kill you, and it makes them feel good. Tell your wives they look good to you, and see if things don't get better. Wives, do the same to your husbands. Love is a caring emotion. If you don't love yourself, it's hard to love your families and hard to love your brothers and sisters in Christ. If love ceases in a marriage, it will fall apart. If love ceases in the church, it will fall apart. **If love ceases in our relationship with Christ, we will fall apart**, for you see, this Christian walk with Jesus is a marriage. Jesus is the Bridegroom, and we are the bride. As long as we have this love affair with Jesus and walk with Him, there will be no occasion to fall.

1 John 2:11

But he that hateth his brother is in darkness, and walketh in darkness, and knoweth not whither he goeth, because that darkness hath blinded his eyes.

In Verse 11, John is still trying to get the saints to realize that they cannot please God with ill feelings or hatred in their lives. **Hatred is a feeling brought by the devil**, because he knows that hatred consumes the heart and life, causing good people to do terrible things. The story is told of a man walking home in the dark; and in the distance he saw a light and wondered who it might be coming to meet him. When the man got close, he saw that the stranger was blind, and he asked the blind man, "Why, being blind, do you carry a light?" The blind man told him, "Well, you see, I carry this light not because I need it, but I carry it so I won't be a stumbling block to someone else."

If we will learn this lesson, the best way to not be a stumbling block is to walk in love toward our Christian brothers and sisters. We are given one of two choices: **we can walk in the light of God's love, or we can walk in darkness away from God**. Those who walk in darkness are lost and blind. They cannot find their way because their eyes are covered with the scales of sin. Child of God, think of how your life was before you met Jesus, and look at it today; see the difference that Jesus can make? Don't be one who just professes to be saved. The world knows how a Christian should act, and they act the act. They know how a Christian should talk, so they talk the talk. However, if there's hatred in their heart, it's all for nothing.

As Christians, we will never agree on everything until we reach heaven, but that doesn't stop the love of God from binding us together. Even in the day of the Apostles, the Apostles looked at some things differently, but their goal was the same: to get as many saved as humanly possible. Our goal should be the same as theirs. But, sometimes we must work out our differences. We need to talk to each other, which sounds easy, but often isn't. If we can reach common ground, there we will find a starting place.

Whether working out church problems or marriage problems, don't stay in the dark where you are blind and cannot see. Come into the light that only God gives, and once in the light, the whole picture changes.

The Wiersbe Bible Commentary gives an example: "A Christian couple came to see a pastor because their marriage was beginning to fall apart. 'We're both saved,' the discouraged husband said, 'but we just aren't happy together. There's no joy in our home.' As the pastor talked with them and they considered together what the Bible has to say, one fact became clear: both the husband and wife were nursing grudges. Each recalled many annoying little things the other had done. 'If you two really loved each other,' said the pastor, 'you wouldn't file these hurts away in your hearts. Grudges fester in our hearts like infected sores and poison the whole system,

"Then he read, '[love] thinketh no evil' (1 Corinthians 13:5). He explained, 'This means that love never keeps records of things others do that hurt us. When we truly love someone, our love covers their sins and helps to heal the wounds they cause.' Then he read, 'And above all things have fervent love among yourselves for love shall cover the multitude of sins' (1 Peter 4:8). Before the couple left, the pastor counseled them: 'Instead of keeping records of the things that hurt, start numbering the things that please. An unforgiving spirit always breeds poison, but a loving spirit that sees and remembers the best always produces health.'"

We cannot afford to let the darkness of this world blind us, not in our everyday walk or in our Christian walk. This Christian walk is the only walk that brings true love and peace. To quote the world, "It's the real thing." The Bible from Genesis to Revelation is full of truth, wisdom and understanding, but the abiding key to this whole thing is to have a Christ-like love, because love heals all wounds. Love sent Jesus to the cross. Did he want to die? No, read the prayer that Jesus prayed in the garden. **Love for you and me, however, sent him to that cross.** Oh, the love of Jesus, to die for me. Oh, the price, the awful price that was paid for man.

1 John 2:12-14

12 I write unto you, little children, because your sins are forgiven you for his name's sake.
13 I write unto you, fathers, because ye have known him that is from the beginning. I write unto you, young men, because ye have overcome the wicked one. I write unto you, little children, because ye have known the Father.
14 I have written unto you, fathers, because ye have known him that is from the beginning. I have written unto you, young men, because ye are strong, and the Word of God abideth in you, and ye have overcome the wicked one.

In these verses, it seems that many Bible theologians believe that John is being overly repetitive. These verses cover exactly the same thing, but it's expressed in different ways. **John's desire is to get people's attention** to explain to them that we must stay in the light of God's love, that we must have an up-to-date, working relationship with the Lord and that it's the only way to stay saved. *The Wiersbe Bible Commentary* explains John's desire to keep saints from evil: "The answer is found in the unusual form of address used in 1 John 2:12-14. Note the titles used as John addresses his Christian readers: little children, fathers, young men, little children. What was he referring to?

"To begin with, 'little children' (1 John 2:12) refers to all believers. Literally, this word means 'born ones.' All Christians have been born into God's family through faith in Jesus Christ, and their sins have been forgiven. The very fact that one is in God's family, sharing His nature, ought to discourage him from becoming friendly with the world. To be friendly with the world is treachery! Friendship of the world is enmity with God, whoever therefore will be [wants to be] a friend of the world is the enemy of God (James 4:4).

"But something else is true: we begin as little children – born ones – but we must not stay that way! Only as a Christian grows spiritually does he overcome the world."

In our churches, there should be, for lack of a better term, different classes. There should be the "Fathers and Mothers," the older more mature Christians, those who should be the examples of Christian love and wisdom for the younger Christians to follow and pattern themselves after. Next are the "young men and women" in their twenties to their fifties; these young men and women are the work force of the church. They should be ready to do whatever is needed to maintain the church and do most of the witnessing to reach the lost, although it is everyone's duty to witness and tell of Jesus' love and grace and mercy. Third are the "children," those whom God has put in our hands to teach and instruct in the ways of God, to nurture and instill in them a love for God, His word and all things that pertain to Him. These young children all the way through their teenage years are the church, should the Lord tarry. **It's our responsibility to see that God has access to their hearts and minds**, to unfold to them this is what the Word says and teaches.

Proverbs 22:6

Train up a child in the way he should go: and when he is old, he will not depart from it.

Ephesians 6:4

And, ye fathers, provoke not your children to wrath: but bring them up in the nurture and admonition of the Lord.

Titus 2:1-8

[1] But speak thou the things which become sound doctrine:
[2] That the aged men be sober, grave, temperate, sound in faith, in charity, in patience.
[3] The aged women likewise, that they be in behaviour as becometh holiness, not false accusers, not given to much wine, teachers of good things;
[4] That they may teach the young women to be sober, to love their husbands, to love their children,
[5] To be discreet, chaste, keepers at home, good, obedient to their own husbands, that the Word of God be not blasphemed.
[6] Young men likewise exhort to be sober minded.
[7] In all things shewing thyself a pattern of good works: in doctrine shewing uncorruptness, gravity, sincerity,
[8] Sound speech, that cannot be condemned; that he that is of the contrary part may be ashamed, having no evil thing to say of you.

The world today does everything it can to seduce God's

people away from the church. To the world, the church should submit to their moral standards, their sense of right and wrong, thus doing away with the Word of God. Sadly, the church world is beginning to crumble under the pressure of the world. All I can say is that many churches are full of cowards trying desperately to maintain their offices as church leaders, while at the same time selling their people down the river and handing them over to the wiles of the devil.

They are not God-called but hirelings and cowards, not caring about God's flock. **The only thing they desire is to fill their own bellies and wants.** However, one day they will stand before God, and God will not deal kindly with them. If there are degrees in hell, then hell will be hotter for them than anybody else. *John Phillips Commentary* gives us a look at this modern church of liberals who bow at the altar of this world.

"What a pitiful 'Christ' the liberals have! Their 'Christ' was not virgin born but was illegitimately born. He performed no miracles, and he was martyred because he was ahead of his time. He did not bodily rise from the dead, and he is not now seated, physically, at God's right hand in heaven, nor is he coming again. Nor is there anything remarkable to them about the Bible, which they view as just another book, one full of errors and contradictions. All these conclusions, hailed as the assured results of so-called 'higher criticism,' are presented with a great show of scholarship. And they are all false."

When people turn away from God, but still want others to think of them as Godly, they will do all manner of things to try and hide, or cover up, their true self. They criticize the Word of God, and they use logic to try and discredit the truth of the Word. They forget that **God doesn't work according to man's logic or his reasoning.** He moves and works according to his own will and desires. A perfect example of a man who has left the truth of God's Word is a self-called preacher in a large city in Texas. He went on nationwide TV and said that he didn't believe everything written in the Bible, that the Bible was wrong to criticize the homosexual life style and that Jesus would have approved of it; that the apostles Paul, Peter and John were wrong for their writings and should be rebuked; that they were misguided and judgmental. He claimed God doesn't judge one sin to be worse than another, and that everybody, all mankind, is going to heaven. This man says there's enough condemnation in the world, and we don't need any more, not even from the Bible.

1 John 2:15

Love not the world, neither the things that are in the world. If any man love the world, the love of the Father is not in him.

The verse begins, *"Love not the world, neither the things that are in the world."* The world can be thought of in three different ways.

1. The world – the world that God created, a beautiful place with seas, mountains, deserts, a truly wonderful place, green trees, blue skies, clouds, the handiwork of God
2. The spiritual world – where good combats evil. Where Satan tries to control the spiritual life of men and women
3. The world of man – a world where man lives according to his nature. A world where hatred, violence, and

cruelty reigns supreme. Where man is pleasure mad, and a desire to own material things overshadows man's need.

This last world is the world that John is speaking about, the world of the here and now. I want it now, because tomorrow I might be dead; the world of "you have it and I want it, so I'll just take it." This mind frame is what John is warning about. We live in this world, but **as born-again children of God, we aren't of this world**. When we accepted Jesus, our spiritual citizenship changed from this world, and we became citizens of God's Kingdom, Heaven.

The world John is telling us not to love is this human world; the world that is arranged and organized by the devil, who is the prince of this world that is so alluring to the saints of God. Drive down the highway in most cities, and you'll find places all lit up in colored lights. Why? To attract passersby to come inside and see what the devil has to offer. In *John Phillips Commentary*, we read the following words:

"John tells us also what a love of the world betrays: 'If any man love the world, the love of the Father is not in him.' (1 John 2:15b). Those who live for this world betray a serious lack of understanding that this world is the enemy of God. John could still hear the earnest voice of the Lord Jesus as it rang through that Jerusalem upper room, praying that His loved ones might be protected from the world, from its attacks and from its attractions. His sheep had been given to Him 'out of the world' (John 17:6) so that now we, as God's people, are in the world but no longer of the world.

"The Lord said bluntly, 'I pray not for the world' (John 17:9), so entrenched was its enmity. Thus, how can we love and admire a system that hates our Beloved? Moreover, the Lord was anticipating an imminent departure from the world: 'Now I am no more in the world, but these are in the world, and I come to thee' (John 17:11). The world's animosity toward the Lord Jesus would soon be transferred to His people."

As we continue to look at the Word, we find that Jesus did not pray that his followers would be raptured out of this world immediately, but that the Father would keep them from evil. **They had a work to do, the work of spreading the gospel, reaching lost souls, building the church, building the kingdom and preparing the bride to meet the Bridegroom.** The world hates us, this we know, but we have been left here to carry on the work that Jesus started until our Heavenly Father says it's enough and tells His Son, Jesus, to "go and get your bride." Let us work while it's day, for the night cometh when no man can work.

1 John 2:16

For all that is in the world, the lust of the flesh, and the lust of the eyes, and the pride of life, is not of the Father, but is of the world.

John now goes into detail and tells us that there are three things in the world that Christians are to be aware of, things that if we're not careful will lure us away from God. That's why it's important to stay prayed up and in constant contact with the Lord. These three groups are:

1. The lust of the flesh
2. The lust of the eyes
3. The pride of life

None of these three groups is of the Father but of the world. Saints, beware, for **the enemy, Satan, is out to destroy God's holy church and us**. The devil tries to find our weak spots, and when he finds them, he hits us there repeatedly. We each and every one have legitimate desires which drive us. God put these into our hearts so that we would desire and strive to attain the perfect will of God. **At the same time, the world knows how to encourage and inflame our desires and tries to turn them into lust.** If we allow the enemy, he will cause us to be consumed by our desires, and this lust will take control of our entire soul and being.

We will be so consumed that nothing will matter to us but fulfilling our fleshly desires. When we speak of fleshly desires, it doesn't have to be sexual; there are other fleshly desires besides adultery, fornication and the like. Overeating is a sin; drinking and getting drunk is a sin of the flesh. These fleshly desires that appeal to Christians are sent by the devil to wean us away from the good things of God and destroy our trust and faith in God.

The next is the lust of the eyes, where the devil puts on a showy appearance to attract the eyes of man away from God. I can tell you from experience that **Satan is very good at his job. He knows just how to make things attractive and appealing.** His merchandise is the best, and it must be to draw the saints' eyes away from God. Solomon is a perfect example. Solomon had riches, anything he wanted, but one of his biggest downfalls was women. He loved women so much that he had seven hundred wives and three hundred concubines; and these wives and concubines were a large part of his downfall with God. Solomon was told not to take wives of the heathen nations, because they would turn his heart away from God. The lust of the eyes is a very entrapping sin.

Proverbs 7:6-27

⁶ For at the window of my house I looked through my casement,

⁷ And beheld among the simple ones, I discerned among the youths, a young man void of understanding,

⁸ Passing through the street near her corner; and he went the way to her house,

⁹ In the twilight, in the evening, in the black and dark night:

¹⁰ And, behold, there met him a woman with the attire of an harlot, and subtil of heart.

¹¹ (She is loud and stubborn; her feet abide not in her house:

¹² Now is she without, now in the streets, and lieth in wait at every corner.)

¹³ So she caught him, and kissed him, and with an impudent face said unto him,

¹⁴ I have peace offerings with me; this day have I payed my vows.

¹⁵ Therefore came I forth to meet thee, diligently to seek thy face, and I have found thee.

¹⁶ I have decked my bed with coverings of tapestry, with carved works, with fine linen of Egypt.

¹⁷ I have perfumed my bed with myrrh, aloes, and cinnamon.

¹⁸ Come, let us take our fill of love until the morning: let us solace ourselves with loves.

¹⁹ For the goodman is not at home, he is gone a long journey:

²⁰ He hath taken a bag of money with him, and will come

home at the day appointed.

21 With her much fair speech she caused him to yield, with the flattering of her lips she forced him.

22 He goeth after her straightway, as an ox goeth to the slaughter, or as a fool to the correction of the stocks;

23 Till a dart strike through his liver; as a bird hasteth to the snare, and knoweth not that it is for his life.

24 Hearken unto me now therefore, O ye children, and attend to the words of my mouth.

25 Let not thine heart decline to her ways, go not astray in her paths.

26 For she hath cast down many wounded: yea, many strong men have been slain by her.

27 Her house is the way to hell, going down to the chambers of death.

Solomon tells us a story that happened as he sat looking out of his window, a story of a young man falling into the snare of the devil. A wanton woman was in the street outside her house, she spies the young man coming toward her. Whereupon she begins to seduce him with her words, painting pretty pictures in his mind. She describes how she picked him out of the crowd. She describes her bed, what her room looks like; she wants him to see all of this in his mind's eye. Then you can also be sure that she uses her body to draw his eyes to her comeliness (beauty). And finally, she leads him into her room. Solomon said in Verse 22: *"He goeth after her straightway, as an ox goeth to the slaughter, or as a fool to the correction of the stocks;"* **The lust of the eyes will lead us astray**, unless we are connected to our Lord and Savior, Jesus Christ.

Another example is Eve. The devil's words were beguiling her, and as she looked at the fruit, she saw that it was desirable.

Genesis 3:6

> *And when the woman saw that the tree was good for food, and that it was pleasant to the eyes, and a tree to be desired to make one wise, she took of the fruit thereof, and did eat, and gave also unto her husband with her; and he did eat.*

Eve lost her spiritual strength and did eat. Adam, on the other hand, **looked at the woman that he loved and desired and yielded to her wiles**, and he did eat. Throughout the pages of the Bible, we read stories of people who looked at various things, desired them and were led astray.

Third and last is the pride of life. **Pride is, perhaps, the original sin.** Pride is what caused Lucifer to be cast out of heaven and down to the earth. Pride is what causes most of the ills of this present world, Lucifer's pride. "Lucifer, how great was thy fall," we read in Isaiah and Ezekiel.

Isaiah 14:12-15

> [12] *How art thou fallen from heaven, O Lucifer, son of the morning! how art thou cut down to the ground, which didst weaken the nations!*
> [13] *For thou hast said in thine heart, I will ascend into heaven, I will exalt my throne above the stars of God: I will sit also upon the mount of the congregation, in the*

sides of the north:

^{14} I will ascend above the heights of the clouds; I will be like the most High.

^{15} Yet thou shalt be brought down to hell, to the sides of the pit.

Ezekiel 28:14-17

^{14} Thou art the anointed cherub that covereth; and I have set thee so: thou wast upon the holy mountain of God; thou hast walked up and down in the midst of the stones of fire.

^{15} Thou wast perfect in thy ways from the day that thou wast created, till iniquity was found in thee.

^{16} By the multitude of thy merchandise they have filled the midst of thee with violence, and thou hast sinned: therefore I will cast thee as profane out of the mountain of God: and I will destroy thee, O covering cherub, from the midst of the stones of fire.

^{17} Thine heart was lifted up because of thy beauty, thou hast corrupted thy wisdom by reason of thy brightness: I will cast thee to the ground, I will lay thee before kings, that they may behold thee.

Pride can and does come in many fashions: the pride of self and personal accomplishments; pride in wealth and power; pride in possessions; pride of race; pride in country. We can be proud of many things, but **we must, we must, learn to keep pride in its proper place and under control**. Remember that pride goes before a fall.

Proverbs 16:18

Pride goeth before destruction, and an haughty spirit before a fall.

In this verse, I would warn against modern Bible scholars as a whole. This new breed of scholars tries to explain away the miracles of the Bible by using logic. Miracles are supernatural and cannot be explained in the natural. **The intellectualism of man cannot explain God's Word, because God's Word is spiritual and must be spiritually discerned.** Man's intelligence is at a total loss when it comes to the moving of God's spirit and power. The scripture tells us that God choses the simple and foolish things to confound the minds of the so-called wise, the intellectuals of this world. But I'd rather know Jesus than to know all that the world knows. *The Weirsbes Commentary* states: "A Christian stays away from the world because of what the world is (a satanic system that hates and opposes Christ), because of what the world does to us (attracts us to live on sinful substitutes), and because of what he (the Christian) is – a child of God."

1 John 2:17

And the world passeth away, and the lust thereof: but he that doeth the will of God abideth for ever.

John, in Verse 17, reminds the saints that this world isn't eternal, and it will one day pass away. This statement will be challenged by the world and even by the modern church. But they are wrong; **they are tied to the devil's scheme of delusion**. We as Christians can be sure of this one thing, that this world will come to an end, just as the Word of God states. There's coming a day when Jesus and His saints will come back to rule and reign over this world, the world governments will cease and the apostate church will no longer exist. We preach and teach that **this world is not our home**, that we, like Abraham, are strangers and pilgrims looking for a city whose builder and maker is God.

John, as one writer states, is speaking of two different kinds of life. One is a life lived for eternity, a life where our heart's desire is to serve God, that one day we might go to dwell with Him forever. The other kind of life is one of time, where we are allotted only so many days, then this body will come to an end. As the song says, "Our days are all numbered down here." A worldly person lives only for the here and now; their world consists of the lust of the flesh, the lust of the eye and the pride of life. They don't know anything else. They've heard about God, but they don't know God. Some don't even believe there is a God, or so they say. I talked with my dad about him fighting in World War II. He was in the navy, a gunner on a merchant marine ship. He told me that he heard men say that they didn't believe in God. But when the enemy planes came in to sink them, and they were trying to shoot them down, everybody was praying. I've found that **when the chips are down, even unbelievers pray**.

It's time that our nation turns once more to God; the enemy is all around us, and only God can save us. Every nation in history that has risen to great heights has fallen because of decadence. We have declined because God is no longer the center of worship. In these last days, it's not enough just to know what the Bible tells us; we need to understand God's will. Many sinners and even so-called Christians know all about Jesus, His life and His miracles; and although they know all about Him, yet they've never met Him on a personal basis.

What are they going to do and say when the rapture takes place and they're still here? That the world has its own personal rapture? It doesn't work that way; there's going to be a rapture of the saints; the dead in Christ are going to rise first, then we which are alive and remain will be caught up to meet them in the air.

1 Thessalonians 4:13-18

13 But I would not have you to be ignorant, brethren, concerning them which are asleep, that ye sorrow not, even as others which have no hope.
14 For if we believe that Jesus died and rose again, even so them also which sleep in Jesus will God bring with him.
15 For this we say unto you by the word of the Lord, that we which are alive and remain unto the coming of the Lord shall not prevent them which are asleep.
16 For the Lord himself shall descend from heaven with a shout, with the voice of the archangel, and with the trump of God: and the dead in Christ shall rise first:
17 Then we which are alive and remain shall be caught up together with them in the clouds, to meet the Lord in the air: and so shall we ever be with the Lord.
18 Wherefore comfort one another with these words.

Child of God, we shall live forever with Christ who died for us; this is the promise which was given to us: that we shall be changed in a moment in the twinkling of an eye, for the trumpet will sound, and scripture states we shall be changed. **Let us therefore be steadfast abounding in the love of God**, putting forth that Christ-like example to this lost and dying world.

1 Corinthians 15:51-58

⁵¹ Behold, I shew you a mystery; We shall not all sleep, but we shall all be changed,

⁵² In a moment, in the twinkling of an eye, at the last trump: for the trumpet shall sound, and the dead shall be raised incorruptible, and we shall be changed.

⁵³ For this corruptible must put on incorruption, and this mortal must put on immortality.

⁵⁴ So when this corruptible shall have put on incorruption, and this mortal shall have put on immortality, then shall be brought to pass the saying that is written, Death is swallowed up in victory.

⁵⁵ O death, where is thy sting? O grave, where is thy victory?

⁵⁶ The sting of death is sin; and the strength of sin is the law.

⁵⁷ But thanks be to God, which giveth us the victory through our Lord Jesus Christ.

⁵⁸ Therefore, my beloved brethren, be ye stedfast, unmoveable, always abounding in the work of the Lord, forasmuch as ye know that your labour is not in vain in the Lord.

1 John 2:18

Little children, it is the last time: and as ye have heard that antichrist shall come, even now are there many antichrists; whereby we know that it is the last time.

John is giving out a warning that these are the last days.

Even though John thought he was already living in the very last days of the church, God in His great mercy has extended time so that we might have the chance to be part of his glorious church.

Ain't God good?

The Wiersbe Bible Commentary states a common belief held today: "It makes no difference what you believe, just as long as you are sincere! That statement expresses the personal philosophy of many people today, but it is doubtful whether most of those who make it have really thought it through. Is sincerity the magic ingredient that makes something true? If so, then you ought to be able to apply it to any area of life, and not only to religion.

"It takes more than sincerity to make something true. Faith in a lie will always cause serious consequences; faith in the truth is never misplaced. It does make a difference what a man believes! If a man wants to drive from Chicago to New York, no amount of sincerity will get him there if the highway is taking him to Los Angeles. A person who is real builds his life on truth, not superstition or lies. It is impossible to live a real life by believing lies."

Sincerity is not enough; passion is not enough. The cults are sincere and have a passion, but **a belief built on lies and fables will never get them to heaven**. There are so many today that have a form of Godliness but deny the full truth of God's Word. They think they are right with God; but men who pervert the gospel for their own personal goals mislead themselves. They cry, send me your tithes, send me an offering, send me so much money and God will meet your need, whatever it is. **We cannot buy God's blessing.** These charlatans are making merchandise of God's people.

Webster's Dictionary defines a charlatan: "a person who

pretends to have expert knowledge or skill that he or she does not have; fake." The radio, TV, and the Internet are full of such people who care only for themselves, and we are a means for them to get what they want. **These fakes are small antichrists preparing the way for the real antichrist to come.**

Please don't get me wrong, not every preacher on TV, radio and the internet is a fake. There are a few real men and women of God, but they are very few. The scriptures speak of a great falling away. This is a falling away from the full truth of God's Word. A large part of this falling away is not just people quitting church, but people who are being led away from the truth by so-called men and women of God who themselves have stopped believing in the full truth of God's Word. **When we become blinded to the truth by Satan, then Satan uses us to lead others away from God.** Anyone who stops accepting the true Word of God becomes an antichrist. This isn't to say we can't have differences among our church family in what we believe. No two Christians believe exactly the same. I'm speaking of those who, for their own gain, change the truth into a lie.

Here are three examples:

The homosexual life style is okay in the sight of God. Not true. It's alright for couples to live together outside of marriage. Again, a lie of the devil. Then there's the preacher who said he didn't believe everything in the Bible, that the apostles were narrow-minded and should be rebuked for what they wrote. This same preacher is leading thousands if not millions straight into Hell. He's an antichrist because he rejects most of the New Testament. **We cannot pick and choose what we want to believe in God's Word**; we must take it all. We are living in the closing days of time before Jesus comes back for his church. Are we ready?

1 John 2:19

They went out from us, but they were not of us; for if they had been of us, they would no doubt have continued with us: but they went out, that they might be made manifest that they were not all of us.

In this verse, John is speaking of what we see occurring today. John is speaking of people who refuse to accept the full truth of the gospel. They leave the church to spread a form of Godliness, but it isn't the full truth of the Word. It isn't enough to walk in the light, and to walk in the precious love of Jesus, but we must also walk in the truth of God's holy word. "Good intentions," as my dad used to say, "don't get the job done." We have a work to do, to reach the lost for Jesus. To do this work, **we must be properly equipped, and that comes by prayer, fasting and studying the Word of God**. We must be prepared to give an answer when asked. A lack of study is one way people get headed down the wrong path. They know just enough to be dangerous to themselves and those around them. They misunderstand the Word, they leave the body and in many cases take others with them. We must remember that when we stand on the true Word of God, we will make some upset and mad, but we must stand for the truth no matter what.

Never have we seen a time when so many people want to believe only part of God's Word and still believe that they will go to heaven when they die. This teaching to be true to your conscience and just be sincere in what you believe isn't enough. **God will not accept anything less than the full truth in what we believe.** That's like saying we don't believe it's wrong to commit adultery, we don't believe it's wrong to steal, we don't believe it's wrong to get drunk or we don't believe it's wrong to cuss, because everybody does it. Just because everybody does it, doesn't make it right in God's sight; and those who say it does are liars, and the truth is not in them. Beware false teachers who seek to deny the truth in God's Word.

1 John 2:20

But ye have an unction from the Holy One, and ye know all things.

Verse 20 tells us that as true believers we have an unction from God. Many will ask, what does it mean when it says unction? *Webster's Dictionary* defines unction as: "the act of anointing as in medical treatment or a religious ceremony," or "a fervent or earnest quality or manner of speaking or behaving, especially in dealing with religious matters." Unction is a special God-given anointing to carry out God's work. There were some people in John's day who claimed to have a special unction from God, which put them on a higher level than most Christians, and that they had been initiated into truths and mysteries beyond the reach of the local church. This, of course, was a lie, for what God has done for one, He will do for all, if we pray earnestly before God. **We as true Christians speak under the anointing of God's spirit**, and the false preachers and teachers speak according to the error of Satan's will. Preacher or teacher, if they teach anything that's contrary to the Bible, God's holy word, they are wrong and do not have the spirit of Christ. God will never go against his own word; to think he would is to be in error.

1 John 2:21

I have not written unto you because ye know not the truth,
but because ye know it, and that no lie is of the truth.

John tells his readers he's not writing to them because they don't know the truth, but because they do know the truth. The Word tells us that the truth will set us free from sin and bondage to this world. **No longer will we be caught in the devil's merry-go-around**, but free in Jesus Christ our Lord. John goes on to tell his readers that no lie is of the truth. No matter how you say it, how you try to put it, a lie is a lie is a lie. You can dress it up, you can put makeup on it, you can put pretty bows on it, you can wash it clean, but a pig is still a pig, just like a lie is still a lie, and you cannot change it. The world does its best and fools a lot of people, but the true child of God still knows the marks of the devil.

The devil will come as an angel of light, even quoting scripture just as he did to Jesus. However, know this: *"Greater is He that is in you than he that is in the world."* Rejoice, for **Jesus has overcome the world**, for they killed Him, and death could not hold Him. They put Him in a grave, and the earth could not hold Him. He is Jesus, the Christ, the only begotten Son of God.

1 John 2:22-23

[22] Who is a liar but he that denieth that Jesus is the Christ?
He is antichrist, that denieth the Father and the Son.
[23] Whosoever denieth the Son, the same hath not the Father: (but) he that acknowledgeth the Son hath the Father also.

These verses explain themselves. Who is a liar, every person who denies that Jesus is the Son of God? Because this is the greatest lie of all time. Scripture tells us that all liars will have their part in the lake of fire. Why? Because God is truth, He is light, and all lies are untruths, thus **all liars cannot enter into the joys of heaven**, into the light of God.

Revelation 21:8

> *But the fearful, and unbelieving, and the abominable, and murderers, and whoremongers, and sorcerers, and idolaters, and all liars, shall have their part in the lake which burneth with fire and brimstone: which is the second death.*

Here I want to insert this: You cannot be a Christian and be a liar. **Liars can have no part in the kingdom of God.** Revelation 21:8 says all liars, and all is inclusive. If you are a liar, you are a sinner. You cannot be saved and be a liar. There are some who say that you have to sin every day, but this is a lie. There are not two classes of liars, the sinner liar and the saved liar. Sin is sin, and all sin will send you to hell.

Ezekiel 18:4

> *Behold, all souls are mine; as the soul of the father, so also the soul of the son is mine: the soul that sinneth, it shall die.*

Ezekiel 18:19-24

> *19 Yet say ye, Why? doth not the son bear the iniquity of*

the father? When the son hath done that which is lawful and right, and hath kept all my statutes, and hath done them, he shall surely live.

20 The soul that sinneth, it shall die. The son shall not bear the iniquity of the father, neither shall the father bear the iniquity of the son: the righteousness of the righteous shall be upon him, and the wickedness of the wicked shall be upon him.

21 But if the wicked will turn from all his sins that he hath committed, and keep all my statutes, and do that which is lawful and right, he shall surely live, he shall not die.

22 All his transgressions that he hath committed, they shall not be mentioned unto him: in his righteousness that he hath done he shall live.

23 Have I any pleasure at all that the wicked should die? saith the Lord GOD: and not that he should return from his ways, and live?

24 But when the righteous turneth away from his right-eousness, and committeth iniquity, and doeth according to all the abominations that the wicked man doeth, shall he live? All his righteousness that he hath done shall not be mentioned: in his trespass that he hath trespassed, and in his sin that he hath sinned, in them shall he die.

Luke 8:11-14

11 Now the parable is this: The seed is the Word of God.

12 Those by the way side are they that hear; then cometh the devil, and taketh away the word out of their hearts, lest they should believe and be saved.

13 They on the rock are they, which, when they hear, re-

ceive the word with joy; and these have no root, which for a while believe, and in time of temptation fall away.

14 And that which fell among thorns are they, which, when they have heard, go forth, and are choked with cares and riches and pleasures of this life, and bring no fruit to perfection.

Luke 9:62

And Jesus said unto him, No man, having put his hand to the plough, and looking back, is fit for the kingdom of God.

Luke 11:24-26

24 When the unclean spirit is gone out of a man, he walketh through dry places, seeking rest; and finding none, he saith, I will return unto my house whence I came out.
25 And when he cometh, he findeth it swept and garnished.
26 Then goeth he, and taketh to him seven other spirits more wicked than himself; and they enter in, and dwell there: and the last state of that man is worse than the first.

Galatians 1:6

I marvel that ye are so soon removed from him that called you into the grace of Christ unto another gospel:

Galatians 4:9

But now, after that ye have known God, or rather are

known of God, how turn ye again to the weak and beggar-
ly elements, whereunto ye desire again to be in bondage?

2 Peter 2:14-15

[14] Having eyes full of adultery, and that cannot cease from
sin; beguiling unstable souls: an heart they have exercised
with covetous practices; cursed children:
[15] Which have forsaken the right way, and are gone astray,
following the way of Balaam the son of Bosor, who loved
the wages of unrighteousness;

2 Peter 2:20-22 (KJV)

[20] For if after they have escaped the pollutions of the world
through the knowledge of the Lord and Saviour Jesus
Christ, they are again entangled therein, and overcome,
the latter end is worse with them than the beginning.
[21] For it had been better for them not to have known the
way of righteousness, than, after they have known it, to
turn from the holy commandment delivered unto them.
[22] But it is happened unto them according to the true prov-
erb, The dog is turned to his own vomit again; and the sow
that was washed to her wallowing in the mire.

Revelation 2:4

Nevertheless I have somewhat against thee, because thou
hast left thy first love.

It makes no difference if you've never been saved, or

you've been saved, turned your back on the good things of God and gone back into the world. **Sin is sin, and sin will send your soul to a very real devil's hell.** John wants us to look at this lie and if there are degrees of lies. The very worst that can be told is the lie of categorically denying that Jesus Christ is the Son of God and our precious Savior. It's time we begin to do like King David and go before God and ask God to restore unto us the joy and the excitement of our salvation.

Psalm 51:11-12

> *[11] Cast me not away from thy presence; and take not thy holy spirit from me.*
> *[12] Restore unto me the joy of thy salvation; and uphold me with thy free spirit.*

The salvation of the Lord brings joy, but it's a joy that must be renewed. It's easy to fall into a rut. One fellow said that a rut is nothing but a grave with both ends opened, and he's right. We get satisfied with things as they are. **It's time to shake things up**, to stir things up in our souls. We must ever strive for the deeper depths and higher heights in God.

There must be a continual desire for all that God has. As we continually pray and study, God opens up new things in His Word to the believers. The person whose desire is the Lord's and what He has is a person who spiritually grows in wisdom and knowledge, for **nothing good will the Lord withhold from His own children**. The question is: how much do we want from God? How much are we willing to give up to receive what we want in God? Oh, God, renew in us continually the joy of your salvation.

1 John 2:24-25

24 Let that therefore abide in you, which ye have heard from the beginning. If that which ye have heard from the beginning shall remain in you, ye also shall continue in the Son, and in the Father.
25 And this is the promise that he hath promised us, even eternal life.

We've combined these two verses as we did in verses 22-23; there's little to say about Verse 24 since it carries the same message as the above scriptures except for one point. John says to let that gospel abide in you, which you heard in the beginning. **If we keep this gospel message, we will remain in the presence of our Lord as His child.** However, he is, at the same time, telling us that there are those who have walked away from the truth and follow different voices. Verse 25 lets us know again that this promise of God is ours if we live for Him, obey His commandments and walk in the light as He is in the light. This promise is ours. We have come too far to give up now, because the end is in sight. Hold fast that which we have in Christ, for we will not be disappointed. Jesus is Lord, and He always will be Lord. The devil can't change it, the end is written and so shall it ever be in Christ Jesus.

1 John 2:26-27

26 These things have I written unto you concerning them that seduce you.
27 But the anointing which ye have received of him abideth in you, and ye need not that any man teach you: but as the

same anointing teacheth you of all things, and is truth, and is no lie, and even as it hath taught you, ye shall abide in him.

John again speaks of the things that he had written unto them, warning them of those who would seduce them, or lead them away from the truth of God's Word. If we look closely at the seducers, they aren't trying to lead sinners into their false teachings; they could care less about the sinners. These false seducers, these anti-Christian groups, rarely ever try to entice the sinners into their cause and their false style of believing. **Their aim, their goal, is to entice the saints away from God's Word and His teachings of living a holy life.**

There are many false groups in the world today. However, two main groups come to mind. They both work fervently to lead the faithful away from the true faith. They both have perverted bibles and go from door to door trying to persuade the Christians that what they believe is wrong and that they know the right path. They are good in their deducing ways and count on most Christians not having a good knowledge of scripture, because sadly, most Christians never study their Bibles at home.

Satan is a liar and the father of lies, according to scripture, and must be rebuked in the name of Jesus. To quote a lengthy paragraph from *The Wiersbe Bible Commentary*:

"Satan is not an originator; he is a counterfeiter. He imitates the work of God. For example, Satan has counterfeit 'ministers' (2 Cor. 11:13-15) who preach a counterfeit gospel (Gal. 1:6-12) that produces counterfeit christians (John 8:43-44) who depend on a counterfeit righteousness (Romans 10:1-10). In the parable of the tares (Matthew 13:24-30, 36-43), Jesus and Satan are pictured as sowers. Jesus sows the true seed, the children of God, but Satan sows 'the children of the wicked one.' The two kinds of plants, while growing, look so much alike that the servants could not tell the difference until the fruit appeared! Satan's chief stratagem during this age is to plant the counterfeit wherever Christ plants the true. And it is important that you be able to detect the counterfeit and separate the teachings of Christ from the false teachings of the antichrist."

The counterfeit gospel is like counterfeit money: it's hard to tell the difference. We must know the signs, what to look for, and most importantly, we must have discernment. Discernment is the first key. God will tell us that something is not quite right, then we begin to look for the small signs that point to the deception. These signs will be very small, just a thought here or there, some small change in the truth. Once that small change has been accepted, then they go on to another small change until they have taken away the power of the truth. It's a simple matter to fully lead believers astray. Every true believer needs the anointing power of God working in his or her life, because **the anointing breaks the yoke of the devil's lies**.

Isaiah 10:27

> *And it shall come to pass in that day, that his burden shall be taken away from off thy shoulder, and his yoke from off thy neck, and the yoke shall be destroyed because of the anointing.*

If the yoke isn't broken, then we are in bondage to the enemy. We can look at bondage like debt. When a person has a large amount of debt, it seems like they are in bondage, and they really are. They are bound and cannot do the things they desire to do. It's like a prison they can't escape from; they are restricted in what they can do. If possible, never ever take on a large amount of debt. It's a bondage the believer doesn't need and doesn't want. Anything that controls us, besides our love and service to the Lord, is a hindrance. **Debt is a heavy burden that weighs on your mind and that you can't escape from.** Don't be a debtor to this world. The Lord is the only one we are to be in debt to.

Remember the anointing breaks the yoke of sin. When we turn our hearts over to the Lord, we receive salvation and God's divine anointing. Use it in your everyday walk with the Lord. **The anointing will reveal the snares of the enemy.** The anointing power of God teaches us how to walk with God; it teaches us the truth of God's Word. It is this teaching force that we need in our lives. This isn't to say that we don't need preachers and teachers, because we most certainly do. We need the Word taught to us; we need preachers to expound the Word to us. The anointing is to reveal to us the truth as we hear and study God's Word, and to also reveal to us when the enemy brings in false teaching to lead us astray. We must abide in the vine and know that all is right between us and God.

John 15:1-11

¹ I am the true vine, and my Father is the husbandman.
² Every branch in me that beareth not fruit he taketh away: and every branch that beareth fruit, he purgeth it, that it may bring forth more fruit.
³ Now ye are clean through the word which I have spoken unto you.
⁴ Abide in me, and I in you. As the branch cannot bear fruit of itself, except it abide in the vine; no more can ye,

except ye abide in me.

⁵ I am the vine, ye are the branches: He that abideth in me, and I in him, the same bringeth forth much fruit: for without me ye can do nothing.

⁶ If a man abide not in me, he is cast forth as a branch, and is withered; and men gather them, and cast them into the fire, and they are burned.

⁷ If ye abide in me, and my words abide in you, ye shall ask what ye will, and it shall be done unto you.

⁸ Herein is my Father glorified, that ye bear much fruit; so shall ye be my disciples.

⁹ As the Father hath loved me, so have I loved you: continue ye in my love.

¹⁰ If ye keep my commandments, ye shall abide in my love; even as I have kept my Father's commandments, and abide in his love.

¹¹ These things have I spoken unto you, that my joy might remain in you, and that your joy might be full.

1 John 2:28-29

²⁸ And now, little children, abide in him; that, when he shall appear, we may have confidence, and not be ashamed before him at his coming.

²⁹ If ye know that he is righteous, ye know that every one that doeth righteousness is born of him.

John again tells us to abide in Christ and let the anointing do its work to keep us safe from harm. Here I need to add this one thing: The anointing reveals to us errors that some preachers and teachers make. However, at the same time we need to know that

there's a difference between spiritual ignorance and outright deception or plain false teaching. Everyone makes mistakes from time to time. False teachers will usually concentrate on one thing over and over until they think they have persuaded you to believe their error, then move to the next falsehood. Anyone who tries to change the meaning of God's Word or just change the Word is wrong.

2 Timothy 3:16-17

16 All scripture is given by inspiration of God, and is profitable for doctrine, for reproof, for correction, for instruction in righteousness:
17 That the man of God may be perfect, thoroughly furnished unto all good works.

Matthew 4:4

But he answered and said, It is written, Man shall not live by bread alone, but by every word that proceedeth out of the mouth of God.

Acts 20:27-30

27 For I have not shunned to declare unto you all the counsel of God.
28 Take heed therefore unto yourselves, and to all the flock, over the which the Holy Ghost hath made you overseers, to feed the church of God, which he hath purchased with his own blood.
29 For I know this, that after my departing shall grievous

wolves enter in among you, not sparing the flock.
[30] Also of your own selves shall men arise, speaking per-
verse things, to draw away disciples after them.

The enemy, as Paul has said, has come in as grievous wolves to destroy the flock of God, preaching and teaching perverse doctrines to draw away the children from the truth. Minister, obey the word; feed the church on the good things of God. Be not deceived by charlatans who would destroy the flock to which God has made you the overseer. We must abide in the truth of the whole Word of God. **The Word is our sword to defeat our enemy.** Learn it and use it, for it's full of powerful truths, from Genesis to Revelation. John Phillips gives us an example of how the Old Testament describes a picture of the bride preparing for the Bridegroom, the return of Jesus:

"The Old Testament contains pictures of New Testament truth, and in Genesis 23 we catch a glimpse of the anticipation of the church in meeting Christ. The father (Abraham) sent his servant (a type of the Holy Spirit) to find a bride for Isaac. He discovered that bride in distant Mesopotamia, and her heart responded at once to the question, 'Wilt thou go with this man?' 'I will,' she said. Then came the journey home. We can picture Rebekah as she plies the servant with questions, wanting to learn all she can about the beloved so as to prepare her heart for the day when she meets him face to face.

"We picture her learning of him. She must have had a thousand questions about the father's well-beloved son, and the servant delighted to fill her mind with thoughts of him. He would not talk much about himself but would direct her thoughts to Isaac. He would tell her all about Moriah and how Isaac became obedient to death and how he did always those things that pleased the father.

"Then we picture her longing for him. As the journey wore on, her life in Mesopotamia would become increasingly a thing of the past, and Isaac would become more and more real. She would think upon his name (laughter) and how he filled his father's heart with joy. Thoughts of him would fill her own heart with joy until, at last, her every thought would be of him.

"Finally, we picture her looking for Isaac. The servant made her increasingly aware the journey was almost over and Isaac would be coming to meet her. She began to give more attention to her toilet and her dress so that, should he come unexpectedly, he would find her ready and with nothing of which to be ashamed.

"If that was so in that far-off day, and in the Old Testament type, how much more it should be characteristic of us today. John would have us 'abide in Christ,' fill our thoughts with thoughts of him, fill our hearts with eager expectation. For the long journey is almost over. Jesus is coming again. Coming suddenly. Coming soon. The Lord's 'be ye therefore ready' is echoed in John's 'be not ashamed of his coming.'"

There are many who profess to be Christians and think they truly are, but they have believed a lie of the devil, and are astray from God. These will be ashamed when Christ shall come. **For Jesus is righteous; and they that serve him, serve him in righteousness and truth, without spot and blemish**, a bride who hath prepared herself to meet her bridegroom. Jesus is our Bridegroom; he is our high priest, our soon-coming king.

Hebrews 7:26

For such an high priest became us, who is holy, harmless,

undefiled, separate from sinners, and made higher than the heavens;

Let us live a life that is righteous before God; let us show forth the praises of him who hath called us into this marvelous light. **To God be the praise for ever and ever.** This life is a question of truth or consequences. If we don't face the truth, we will pay the consequences.

Chapter 2 – Test Your Knowledge

1. What is sin?

_____

_____

2. Who is He?

_____

3. If we do sin, we have an

_____

4. What is the reason most people are led astray?

_____

_____

5. Is it possible to live a perfect life in the sight of God?

_____

6. How are we made overcomers?

_____

_____

_____

7. How do we show the world that we know Jesus?

_____

_____

8. Will a backslidden person go to heaven?

_____

9. In 1st John, John deals with three main things, which are

_____

_____

_____

10. Trust in God equals

_____

_____

11. It is vital that we learn to separate sin from

_____

12. If Jesus is the Bridegroom then who is the bride?

_____

13. Love heals all

_____

14. There are three classes of people in the church. What are they?

_____

_____

_____

15. The church people who are in the twenty through the fif-ties age group are the

_____

16. If you train up a child in the ways of the Lord, they will not depart from it when?

_____

17. We are told in Verse 15 to love not

_____

_____

18. What three things does John say are in the world?

_____

_____

_____

19. Like Abraham we are looking for

_____

_____

20. A worldly person only lives for

_____

_____

21. What do we get from the Holy Ghost?

_____

_____

22. What is an unction?

_____

_____

23. Who is a liar?

_____

_____

24. What did King David ask God to restore?

_____

_____

25. What is the promise that we have been promised?

_____

_____

26. What is the seducer's aim or goal?

_____

_____

27. Do the seducers care about sinners?

_____

28. In the parable of the sower, Jesus and the devil are both

portrayed as _____

29. What breaks the yoke?

_____

30. The Old Testament story of Isaac and Rebekah is a picture

of the _____

_____

31. If we do not face the truth we will

_____

_____

Chapter 3

1 John 3:1

Behold, what manner of love the Father hath bestowed upon us, that we should be called the sons of God: therefore the world knoweth us not, because it knew him not.

In Verse 1, John begins to tell us of the son-ship of God, that as we live for and walk with God, we are called the sons of God. John impresses upon us **how grateful we should be to have the love of God given unto us**, who are unworthy to even call upon the name of God. Yet, He loves us; from the creation He has loved us; when we were unlovable, He loved us. Oh, the precious love of God that extends to man. If we really take time to think about the love of God and what it means, the plan of salvation was worked out before the creation. Why then did God do it? Because He knew there would be those who would love Him and worship Him, and in His love, He deemed that the sacrifice was not too great.

This is the love of God that He has given, that Jesus paid the price for our redemption, and that we, through the blood of Jesus, have been brought into the family of God. **We are the sons of God, heirs and joint heirs with Jesus Christ our Lord.** Because of this act of God upon our lives, the world doesn't know us, as it didn't know Jesus, the Savior of this world. In *Barnes' Notes on the Bible*, we read the following:

" 'Behold what manner of love.' What love in kind and in degree. In kind the most tender and the most ennobling, in adopting us into his family, and in permitting us to address him as our Father; in degree the most exalted since there is no higher love that can be shown than in adopting a poor and friendless orphan, and giving him a parent and a home. Even God could bestow upon us no more valuable token of affection than that we should be adopted into his family, and permitted to regard him as our Father. When we remember how insignificant we are as creatures, and how ungrateful, rebellious, and vile we have been as sinners, we may well be amazed at the love which would adopt us into the holy family of God, so that we may be regarded and treated as the children of the Most High."

Romans 8:14-19

14 For as many as are led by the Spirit of God, they are the sons of God.

15 For ye have not received the spirit of bondage again to fear; but ye have received the Spirit of adoption, whereby we cry, Abba, Father.

16 The Spirit itself beareth witness with our spirit, that we are the children of God:

17 And if children, then heirs; heirs of God, and joint-heirs with Christ; if so be that we suffer with him, that we may be also glorified together.

18 For I reckon that the sufferings of this present time are not worthy to be compared with the glory which shall be revealed in us.

[19] For the earnest expectation of the creature waiteth for the manifestation of the sons of God.

We are the sons and daughters of God. What greater gift could we receive than to be part of God's family?

1 John 3:2

Beloved, now are we the sons of God, and it doth not yet appear what we shall be: but we know that, when he shall appear, we shall be like him; for we shall see him as he is.

Again we say unto you that we who are saved by the blood of Jesus, beloved, we are now the true sons and daughters of God. Jesus has paid the price; the agreement is sealed by the blood, and it is finished. We are adopted into the family. **We now have the legal right to call God our precious Father.** Can there be any greater blessing than to be the beloved children of the Father, to be the bride of Christ? If this doesn't stir our hearts, then we are spiritually numb or dead. We are the children of God with all the rights and privileges of a member of God's family. Don't get me wrong, we don't become gods. There's a group that believes that at salvation, they become little gods under the Lord God. This belief is so wrong. They are taking scripture and twisting it to try and build for themselves some sort of foundation for their belief. But their foundation is weak and, like all false foundations, will crumble before God.

Let's look for a moment at this family, the family of God.

There are three ways a person can become part of a family:

1. They can be born in a family by the parents, the natural way.
2. They can marry into a family whereby the husband and wife become part of each other's family.
3. They can be adopted into a family with all the rights and privileges as if they were natural-born.

Now look at what God has done for us who once were sinners.

1. When we repented of our sins and asked for forgiveness, we were born again into the family of God.
2. We were brought into God's family by adoption, the wild olive branch grafted into the family of God. The Word tells us that we have become heirs and joint heirs with Jesus Christ. We have all the rights and privileges of natural-born children.
3. We will become even further bound into the family of God by marriage, for we are the bride of Christ. All we are waiting for is the return of the Bridegroom to take us to the marriage, then to share at the marriage supper of the Lamb.

God is covering all the bases. There's no other way that we can become a member of God's family. We're bound by birth, by adoption and by marriage. How great is our God, our Father!

What will we be like in the great by-and-by? We're not exactly sure, but we know that **whatever Jesus is like, we'll be like Him**. When Jesus rose from the grave, He had a glorified body. He was recognized as Jesus on this earth, but in heaven where the glory of God doth shine, one thing I know, and that is the saints will know Him and be like Him. This is a promise in God's Word.

1 Corinthians 15:35-58

[35] But some man will say, How are the dead raised up? and with what body do they come?

[36] Thou fool, that which thou sowest is not quickened, except it die:

[37] And that which thou sowest, thou sowest not that body that shall be, but bare grain, it may chance of wheat, or of some other grain:

[38] But God giveth it a body as it hath pleased him, and to every seed his own body.

[39] All flesh is not the same flesh: but there is one kind of flesh of men, another flesh of beasts, another of fishes, and another of birds.

[40] There are also celestial bodies, and bodies terrestrial: but the glory of the celestial is one, and the glory of the terrestrial is another.

[41] There is one glory of the sun, and another glory of the moon, and another glory of the stars: for one star differeth from another star in glory.

[42] So also is the resurrection of the dead. It is sown in corruption; it is raised in incorruption:

[43] It is sown in dishonour; it is raised in glory: it is sown in weakness; it is raised in power:

[44] It is sown a natural body; it is raised a spiritual body. There is a natural body, and there is a spiritual body.

^{45} *And so it is written, The first man Adam was made a living soul; the last Adam was made a quickening spirit.*

^{46} *Howbeit that was not first which is spiritual, but that which is natural; and afterward that which is spiritual.*

^{47} *The first man is of the earth, earthy: the second man is the Lord from heaven.*

^{48} *As is the earthy, such are they also that are earthy: and as is the heavenly, such are they also that are heavenly.*

^{49} *And as we have borne the image of the earthy, we shall also bear the image of the heavenly.*

^{50} *Now this I say, brethren, that flesh and blood cannot inherit the kingdom of God; neither doth corruption inherit incorruption.*

^{51} *Behold, I shew you a mystery; We shall not all sleep, but we shall all be changed,*

^{52} *In a moment, in the twinkling of an eye, at the last trump: for the trumpet shall sound, and the dead shall be raised incorruptible, and we shall be changed.*

^{53} *For this corruptible must put on incorruption, and this mortal must put on immortality.*

^{54} *So when this corruptible shall have put on incorruption, and this mortal shall have put on immortality, then shall be brought to pass the saying that is written, Death is swallowed up in victory.*

^{55} *O death, where is thy sting? O grave, where is thy victory?*

^{56} *The sting of death is sin; and the strength of sin is the law.*

^{57} *But thanks be to God, which giveth us the victory through our Lord Jesus Christ.*

^{58} *Therefore, my beloved brethren, be ye stedfast, unmove-*

able, always abounding in the work of the Lord, foras-much as ye know that your labour is not in vain in the Lord.

We shall see Jesus, and we shall know Him. We shall hear His voice, and we shall follow Him wherever He goes, for He is the Lord. I will praise Him in the morning, I will praise Him in the noontime, I will praise Him when the sun goes down.

1 John 3:3

And every man that hath this hope in him purifieth himself, even as he is pure.

John continues in this verse to promote that we need to have this blessed hope burning within our souls. This blessed hope inspires the Christian to strive to be like Jesus in word, actions, and spirit. Some say that it's impossible to be like Jesus, but I contend that it isn't.

We, you and I, can and must live a perfect life in the sight of God. Not in the sight of man, for that's impossible. **Man always looks for and tries to find fault.** How many scriptures in the Word of God talk and stress that the saints, the children of God, need to strive to be perfect? If it's impossible and can't be done, then why does the Word call for it?

Let us look at what the Word says.

Matthew 5:48

Be ye therefore perfect, even as your Father which is in heaven is perfect.

Matthew 19:21

Jesus said unto him, If thou wilt be perfect, go and sell that thou hast, and give to the poor, and thou shalt have treasure in heaven: and come and follow me.

Luke 6:40

The disciple is not above his master: but every one that is perfect shall be as his master.

John 17:23

I in them, and thou in me, that they may be made perfect in one; and that the world may know that thou hast sent me, and hast loved them, as thou hast loved me.

1 Corinthians 2:4-6

[4] And my speech and my preaching was not with enticing words of man's wisdom, but in demonstration of the Spirit and of power:
[5] That your faith should not stand in the wisdom of men, but in the power of God.
[6] Howbeit we speak wisdom among them that are perfect: yet not the wisdom of this world, nor of the princes of this world, that come to nought:

2 Corinthians 13:9-11

[9] For we are glad, when we are weak, and ye are strong:

and this also we wish, even your perfection.

[10] Therefore I write these things being absent, lest being present I should use sharpness, according to the power which the Lord hath given me to edification, and not to destruction.

[11] Finally, brethren, farewell. Be perfect, be of good comfort, be of one mind, live in peace; and the God of love and peace shall be with you.

Ephesians 4:11-13

[11] And he gave some, apostles; and some, prophets; and some, evangelists; and some, pastors and teachers;

[12] For the perfecting of the saints, for the work of the ministry, for the edifying of the body of Christ:

[13] Till we all come in the unity of the faith, and of the knowledge of the Son of God, unto a perfect man, unto the measure of the stature of the fulness of Christ:

Philippians 3:14-15

[14] I press toward the mark for the prize of the high calling of God in Christ Jesus. [15] Let us therefore, as many as be perfect, be thus minded: and if in any thing ye be otherwise minded, God shall reveal even this unto you.

Colossians 1:28

Whom we preach, warning every man, and teaching every man in all wisdom; that we may present every man perfect in Christ Jesus:

Colossians 4:12

Epaphras, who is one of you, a servant of Christ, saluteth you, always labouring fervently for you in prayers, that ye may stand perfect and complete in all the will of God.

2 Timothy 3:16-17

[16] All scripture is given by inspiration of God, and is profitable for doctrine, for reproof, for correction, for instruction in righteousness: [17] That the man of God may be perfect, thoroughly furnished unto all good works.

Hebrews 6:1

Therefore leaving the principles of the doctrine of Christ, let us go on unto perfection; not laying again the foundation of repentance from dead works, and of faith toward God,

Hebrews 12:23

To the general assembly and church of the firstborn, which are written in heaven, and to God the Judge of all, and to the spirits of just men made perfect,

Hebrews 13:20-21

[20] Now the God of peace, that brought again from the dead our Lord Jesus, that great shepherd of the sheep, through the blood of the everlasting covenant,

²¹ Make you perfect in every good work to do his will, working in you that which is wellpleasing in his sight, through Jesus Christ; to whom be glory for ever and ever. Amen.

James 3:2

For in many things we offend all. If any man offend not in word, the same is a perfect man, and able also to bridle the whole body.

These scriptures deal with man through the grace and power of God about being able to live a perfect life in the sight of God. **We cannot live it within ourselves; we must let Jesus live through us; it's the only way.** The scripture tells us further that if we do sin, we have an advocate with the Father, Jesus Christ the righteous.

Churches need to teach their people that it isn't a sin to be tempted. Sin comes when we yield to the temptation. Every Christian is going to be tempted by the devil; Jesus was tempted of the devil, but He never yielded to the temptation and thus He never sinned. To quote one preacher: "You can't stop the birds from flying over your head, but you don't have to let them nest in your hair." Churches need to wake up. If the devil puts a thought into a person's head, that isn't a sin. It's a temptation. **Sin comes when we put that thought in action.** If we rebuke the devil, submit ourselves to Jesus and put that thought out of our minds, there's no sin. Most people including preachers and teachers do not know the difference between temptation and sin. We must study the Word.

1 John 2:1

My little children, these things write I unto you, that ye sin not. And if any man sin, we have an advocate with the Father, Jesus Christ the righteous:

1 John 3:4-6

[4] Whosoever committeth sin transgresseth also the law: for sin is the transgression of the law.
[5] And ye know that he was manifested to take away our sins; and in him is no sin.
[6] Whosoever abideth in him sinneth not: whosoever sinneth hath not seen him, neither known him.

The apostle wants people to live a righteous life before God. There was a teaching that taught the people that they could sin and still be a Christian. All through the New Testament scripture, it teaches that the soul that sinneth shall die. John taught that all sin goes against God's law; that those who sin are of the devil and not true believers. John states that whosoever sins, transgresses the law. As we look at this statement, understand that **we live under grace and not the law**. The law under Moses, of blood sacrifice, was done away with when Jesus came and fulfilled the law. But the law or the rules God has set for pure and righteous living are still the same. The Ten Commandments have not become the ten suggestions. **The Ten Commandments are still commandments that we are to live by**; they are rules God has set for righteous living and haven't changed.

People seek ways to ease their conscience because of how they live. If we seek the path of righteousness before God, we must live a life of obedience. **God has never asked us to do anything that would harm or hurt us.** He loves us more than we can imagine. We must realize that we serve God because we love Him and not because we fear Him. Yes, scripture teaches that the fear of the Lord is the beginning of wisdom. I repented and asked God to forgive me of my sin, because I didn't want to die and go to a devil's hell. But, when Jesus came into my heart, He replaced that fear with such a love as I have never known. The law of God is given to define what sin is. There must be a dividing point as to what sin is and what sin is not. This dividing point is the law of God. When Jesus came to fulfill the law, he came to set us free from the burden of sin. This Jesus, God's only Son, was made manifest for us, for our profit. His death was to take the sins of this world upon himself that we might become free. **Salvation is free to whosoever will, but we must accept it**, or it does us no good.

John was a man used greatly by God. I believe that John felt overwhelmed by all he had seen, experienced and gone through. He was called by Jesus to walk and talk with Him, to be on the mountain when Jesus was transfigured and the glory of God was made manifest, to be with Jesus after John was raised from the dead and watch as Jesus was taken from their midst back into heaven. He heard the angels tell them that this same Jesus would one day return in like manner to catch away His bride. He suffered persecution at the hands of the Romans, and now in his old age, he was very much aware that Satan was trying to destroy the church, not only from the outside but also from the inside.

John tells us again and again that Jesus was a man with no sin, for He is the light; in Him is no darkness, for Jesus is the One, the only begotten Son of God. We strive to live a pure and holy life in the sight of God. At times, we may fall, but the greatest failure is to wallow in pity. So, **get up, ask forgiveness and walk on with Jesus**.

Read the message in the words of J. Denham Smith in his song:

Rise, My Soul! Behold 'tis Jesus

Rise, my soul! Behold 'tis Jesus,
Jesus fills thy wond'ring eyes;
See Him now in glory seated,
Where thy sins no more can rise.

There in righteousness transcendent,
Lo! He doth in heaven appear,
Shows the blood of His atonement
As thy title to be there.

All thy sins were laid upon Him,
Jesus bore them on the tree;
God, who knew them, laid them on Him,
And, believing, thou art free.

1 John 3:6-7

⁶ Whosoever abideth in him sinneth not: whosoever sin-
neth hath not seen him, neither known him.
⁷ Little children, let no man deceive you: he that doeth
righteousness is righteous, even as he is righteous.

John is again pushing the point that *"whosoever abideth in*

Jesus sinneth not." The nature of God is good through an ever-lasting love that He has for man. If we purpose in our heart and set our will on serving God, we will not sin against Him, because sin is to go against God's will and purpose for our lives. John in this verse isn't saying that a Christian cannot sin in this life, but that **a true believer who has set his mind and will on making heaven his home and seeing Jesus face to face won't deliberately sin against God**. John is trying to put what he's saying in such a way that everyone will strive to reach that place where sin and temptation won't affect the child of God.

The Wiersbe Bible Commentary tells us the following: "Sin is basically a matter of the will. For us to assert our will against God's will is rebellion, and rebellion is the root of sin. It is not simply that sin reveals itself in lawless behavior, but that the very essence of sin is lawlessness. No matter what his outward actions may be, a sinner's inward attitude is one of rebellion.

"Little Judy was riding in the car with her father. She decided to stand up in the front seat. Her father commanded her to sit down and put on the seat belt, but she declined. He told her a second time, and again she refused. 'If you don't sit down immediately, I'll pull over to the side of the road and spank you!' Dad finally said, and at this the little girl obeyed. But in a few minutes she said quietly, 'Daddy, I'm still standing up inside.' Lawlessness! Rebellion! Even though there was constraint from the outside, there was still rebellion on the inside, and this attitude is the essence of sin."

Can a person backslide and once again be entangled in the web of sin? Yes, if there's any rebellion in the heart. There was a person who lived a consistent Christian life, his wife died, and he blamed God. He left the church, went back into sin, and he was worse than before he was saved. He died lost and without

God. Some will try to say he was never really saved. That old excuse won't hold, because this man was saved his whole life, he was changed and he happily served God. But because God did not answer his prayers the way he wanted them answered, he walked away from God.

Galatians 4:9

> *But now, after that ye have known God, or rather are known of God, how turn ye again to the weak and beggarly elements, whereunto ye desire again to be in bondage?*

1 Timothy 4:1-2

> *[1] Now the Spirit speaketh expressly, that in the latter times some shall depart from the faith, giving heed to seducing spirits, and doctrines of devils;*
> *[2] Speaking lies in hypocrisy; having their conscience seared with a hot iron;.*

2 Peter 2:20-22

> *[20] For if after they have escaped the pollutions of the world through the knowledge of the Lord and Saviour Jesus Christ, they are again entangled therein, and overcome, the latter end is worse with them than the beginning.*
> *[21] For it had been better for them not to have known the way of righteousness, than, after they have known it, to turn from the holy commandment delivered unto them.*
> *[22] But it is happened unto them according to the true proverb, The dog is turned to his own vomit again; and the sow*

that was washed to her wallowing in the mire.

Whatever the reason or excuse we use, it doesn't satisfy God. God loves us, He made us, but He will not force us to serve Him. We must serve God because we desire to. Satan tries to change our desires from God to the world, but Satan cannot force us to leave God. **If we walk away from God, it's because of our own youthful lust.** God won't make us serve Him, and the devil can't make us serve him. We serve the one we choose. We can blame no one for our actions but ourselves.

John calls us little children probably because he was very old. He warns that we are to let no man deceive us. If we do righteousness, then we are righteous, even as Jesus our Lord is righteous. The Word says that we can know a tree by the fruits it puts forth.

1 John 3:8

[8] He that committeth sin is of the devil; for the devil sinneth from the beginning. For this purpose the Son of God was manifested, that he might destroy the works of the devil.

Scripture states, *"He that committeth sin is of the devil."* **Sin is the act of disobeying God's law.** These rules were put in place to show men and women where the boundary lines are. In every society, in every club, in every organization there must be rules of conduct; so it is with God. God has His rules, and to break these rules is sin. **The soul that sinneth, it shall die.** God has given us the opportunity to escape the punishment of sin. We have the plan of salvation set before us, the way to change our futures. However, the decision is ours to make; no one can make it for us. God loves us, the devil hates us, so what's so hard?

Yet, it is one of the hardest decisions we will ever make. We know what we have, and we live in it every day. What God offers is new and strange, or so we think. Little do we know about the peace we've never had; little do we know of a Godly love, because we've never felt it. **That first step toward God is the hardest step we will ever make and take**, but after that first step, the rest gets easier. And at the end of that short walk toward God is peace like we have never known and a love that passes all understanding. The good part about it is that the world didn't give it to us, and **the world sure can't take it away**.

Sin is a choice, a matter of will. We must set our will to serve God. We'll find life to be much easier and full of joy. John goes on to say that the devil sinneth from the beginning. There are some who say that sin originated with the devil. I can't say yea or nay; all I know is what scripture says.

Isaiah 14:12-15

> [12] *How art thou fallen from heaven, O Lucifer, son of the morning! how art thou cut down to the ground, which didst weaken the nations!*
>
> [13] *For thou hast said in thine heart, I will ascend into heaven, I will exalt my throne above the stars of God: I will sit also upon the mount of the congregation, in the sides of the north:*
>
> [14] *I will ascend above the heights of the clouds; I will be like the most High.*
>
> [15] *Yet thou shalt be brought down to hell, to the sides of the pit.*

Luke 10:18

18 And he said unto them, I beheld Satan as lightning fall from heaven.

Ezekiel 28:14-17

14 Thou art the anointed cherub that covereth; and I have set thee so: thou wast upon the holy mountain of God; thou hast walked up and down in the midst of the stones of fire.

15 Thou wast perfect in thy ways from the day that thou wast created, till iniquity was found in thee.

16 By the multitude of thy merchandise they have filled the midst of thee with violence, and thou hast sinned: therefore I will cast thee as profane out of the mountain of God: and I will destroy thee, O covering cherub, from the midst of the stones of fire.

17 Thine heart was lifted up because of thy beauty, thou hast corrupted thy wisdom by reason of thy brightness: I will cast thee to the ground, I will lay thee before kings, that they may behold thee.

Revelation 12:3-4

3 And there appeared another wonder in heaven; and behold a great red dragon, having seven heads and ten horns, and seven crowns upon his heads.

4 And his tail drew the third part of the stars of heaven, and did cast them to the earth: and the dragon stood be-

fore the woman which was ready to be delivered, for to devour her child as soon as it was born.

Self-pride, self-importance, all goes before a fall. **Lucifer sinned because he desired to be equal with God and even greater than God.** However, he forgot one important thing; he is a created being, made by God. As the world says, when we get too big for our britches, we get ourselves in trouble. This is the reason Jesus came to offer us a way of escape from foolish pride and the other sins that control our lives. Jesus made the way; what we do with it is up to us.

1 John 3:9-10

[9] Whosoever is born of God doth not commit sin; for his seed remaineth in him: and he cannot sin, because he is born of God.
[10] In this the children of God are manifest, and the children of the devil: whosoever doeth not righteousness is not of God, neither he that loveth not his brother.

John continually repeats the same thing over and over, just in different ways. The meaning is the same. Whosoever is born of God does not practice sin. The practitioner of sin is not saved. To practice sin is to deny the saving power of God. There was a group spreading in the churches; this group taught that since Jesus died to cover all sin, once they accepted Christ as their Savior, they could live and do as they pleased, because they were free from sin. To the hearer, this teaching sounded ideal; profess Christ as Lord and Savior, and they were free to do and say whatever they pleased, because they couldn't sin. If they did sin, they simply lost their reward in heaven, but they still had eternal security. That sounds perfect, but it just isn't so. **The only eternal security is to get saved and stay saved**, by living for God every moment of the day. When temptation comes, submit yourself unto God, resist the devil and he will flee from you. That's scripture.

James 4:7

> *Submit yourselves therefore to God. Resist the devil, and he will flee from you.*

1 Peter 5:8-9

> *[8] Be sober, be vigilant; because your adversary the devil, as a roaring lion, walketh about, seeking whom he may devour:*
> *[9] Whom resist stedfast in the faith, knowing that the same afflictions are accomplished in your brethren that are in the world.*

We must, and again I say, must know the Word of God, for the Word is as a sharp, two-edged sword. The Word and a consistent prayer life will keep us from sin. **We must feed our inner man on the Word of God.** *Wiersbe* gives this example: "A converted Native American explained, 'I have two dogs living in me – a mean dog and a good dog. They are always fighting. The mean dog wants me to do bad things, and the good dog wants me to do good things. Do you want to know which dog wins? The one I feed the most.'

"A Christian who feeds the new nature from the Word of God will have power to live a godly life. We are to 'make not provision for the flesh, to fulfill the lust thereof.' (Romans 13:14)."

The false teaching in John's day reminds me of what is being preached in many churches today. What was being taught in the churches was that a Christian didn't have to worry about sin. Once they were saved, only the body sinned, not the spirit. The body could in no way affect the spirit man. Some even taught that it was natural for the body to sin, because the body had been sinful from the very beginning.

As we look at this teaching, we must remember that the body is only a vessel to be used. **The spirit man, which dwells in the body, has control over what's done in the body.** This is why the old man of sin must die, and the new man in Christ Jesus takes his place. Whoever is in control dictates what the body does. This is the reason we must pray daily, and read and study God's Word daily, to feed the spiritual man that he might be pleasing to God and walk after the good things of God. As we feed this new man, God works on us to produce the outward signs of our experience, that those around us might see and know that there has been a complete change in our lives. The harshness is gone; the inclination to do worldly things is gone. We no longer seek to satisfy the lustful temptations the devil brings before us. Our heart's desire is to do the will of God and see others receive what we have received from God.

1 John 3:11-13

[11] For this is the message that ye heard from the beginning, that we should love one another.
[12] Not as Cain, who was of that wicked one, and slew his brother. And wherefore slew he him? Because his own

works were evil, and his brother's righteous.
[13] Marvel not, my brethren, if the world hate you.

John's letter concentrates on the same three points, and they are love, obedience, and truth. We must have a Godly love, we must walk in truth that our light will shine into the darkness, and we must be obedient to the Word of God. For by these three, the love of God is shed abroad to a lost and dying world.

The first thing a person learns when they come in contact with Jesus is his precious and gentle love. True love is kind and gentle. However, **where hatred and malice abound, there is no love**. Remember Cain and Abel, how Cain committed the first recorded murder. There came a time when Cain and Abel brought an offering to God. Abel brought a lamb, a perfect lamb, and sacrificed it before God, for Abel was a shepherd. Cain also brought a sacrifice, but his sacrifice was of the fruit of the ground, for he was a tiller of the ground.

God had respect for Abel's offering, but not Cain's, because **without the shedding of blood, there is no remission of sin**. Scholars say Cain knew God's requirement. When Adam and Eve sinned in the garden, and God came to them, they admitted that they sinned. God then killed animals and shed their blood to make clothes of skins for Adam and Eve. It's believed that this practice of shedding of blood was carried on after they were ejected from the garden; so, Cain and Abel both knew what was required.

Abel complied, but Cain, in rebellion, refused, and so God wouldn't accept his offering. Cain became very angry, and his anger turned into hate; whereupon, he killed his brother, Abel. The Word warns us to not let the sun go down upon our anger. To quote *Wiersbe*: "Christ shows up the world's sin and reveals its true nature. When the world, like Cain,, comes face-to-face with reality and truth, it can make only one of two decisions: repent and change, or destroy the one who is exposing it."

Genesis 4:1-16

¹ And Adam knew Eve his wife; and she conceived, and bare Cain, and said, I have gotten a man from the LORD.
² And she again bare his brother Abel. And Abel was a keeper of sheep, but Cain was a tiller of the ground.
³ And in process of time it came to pass, that Cain brought of the fruit of the ground an offering unto the LORD.
⁴ And Abel, he also brought of the firstlings of his flock and of the fat thereof. And the LORD had respect unto Abel and to his offering:
⁵ But unto Cain and to his offering he had not respect. And Cain was very wroth, and his countenance fell.
⁶ And the LORD said unto Cain, Why art thou wroth? and why is thy countenance fallen?
⁷ If thou doest well, shalt thou not be accepted? and if thou doest not well, sin lieth at the door. And unto thee shall be his desire, and thou shalt rule over him.
⁸ And Cain talked with Abel his brother: and it came to pass, when they were in the field, that Cain rose up against Abel his brother, and slew him.
⁹ And the LORD said unto Cain, Where is Abel thy brother? And he said, I know not: Am I my brother's keeper?
¹⁰ And he said, What hast thou done? the voice of thy brother's blood crieth unto me from the ground.
¹¹ And now art thou cursed from the earth, which hath opened her mouth to receive thy brother's blood from thy

hand;

¹² When thou tillest the ground, it shall not henceforth yield unto thee her strength; a fugitive and a vagabond shalt thou be in the earth.

¹³ And Cain said unto the LORD, My punishment is greater than I can bear.

¹⁴ Behold, thou hast driven me out this day from the face of the earth; and from thy face shall I be hid; and I shall be a fugitive and a vagabond in the earth; and it shall come to pass, that every one that findeth me shall slay me.

¹⁵ And the LORD said unto him, Therefore whosoever slayeth Cain, vengeance shall be taken on him sevenfold. And the LORD set a mark upon Cain, lest any finding him should kill him.

¹⁶ And Cain went out from the presence of the LORD, and dwelt in the land of Nod, on the east of Eden.

Hate is of the world, while love is a product of God. We, as Christian brothers and sisters, must show forth a Christ-like love, even to those who hate us. As Christians, we will face persecution, but Jesus gives us grace.

1 John 3:14-15

¹⁴ We know that we have passed from death unto life, because we love the brethren. He that loveth not his brother abideth in death.

¹⁵ Whosoever hateth his brother is a murderer: and ye know that no murderer hath eternal life abiding in him.

The love of God is strong to the world, for the love of God

brings all sorts of people into the family of God. They can be young or old, rich or poor, man or woman. It makes no difference; we are all the family of God. Black, white, brown, yellow or red, we are one family united in love. Love does not separate; it binds together the children of God. The world hates and despises that which is truly good. Why? **The love of God brings conviction to the hearts of sinners and shows them just how wrong they really are.** The world makes a show of how they accept us and praise our good works. But inwardly, they seek ways to destroy us and the gospel we hold so dear. What the devil has done outwardly, he's now also trying to do inwardly. Little by little, he's finding weak preachers to do his bidding. They have begun to question the Bible. Some have been so bold as to denounce the apostles who wrote the Word as overbearing, hardnosed men who should be rebuked for what they wrote.

When men of today claim to know more of what the Bible says than the apostles, the men who walked and talked with Jesus, were taught by Jesus on how things should be, and wrote what Jesus taught them, they are overstepping their bounds and will pay God's penalty for their conceit. They have become so full of self and self-esteem that they put themselves on the same level as God.

May God help us when turncoat preachers and teachers bow before the devil's altar and submit themselves to the devil's service. These men and women will stand before a just and righteous God and hear Him say, "Depart from me ye workers of iniquity." When scripture states that God will have a remnant, that's what we have today. **With people falling away from the truth, only a remnant is now left.** This great falling away is taking place right before our eyes.

Yes, the churches are losing members faster than ever before, but this is only a part of that falling away. The worst part is all of these fake preachers and teachers perverting the truth of God's Word and convincing Christians to follow them in their misguided truths and ways. To see why, we must go back seventy to eighty years and look at the church then and now.

The greatest danger in the churches is ignorance of God's Word. God has said in His word that He is the same yesterday, today, and forever, that He does not change. The preaching of God's Word is simple; we preach thus sayeth the Lord and preach God's Word just like it is. Preachers today get their sermons out of the newspaper, off of the T.V. and as one preacher said, off the Internet. It sounds like it, too.

What ever happened to preachers praying for God to give them a message to preach? A message for this present time and hour, oh, wait, that means they'll have to study and pray. God forbid that preachers study and pray. **The ministry isn't a life of ease; it's a life of service to God and his people.** Ministers years ago went into the ministry because they were "called" by God. They knew that the labor would be hard, the hours long and the money little to none. However, they were called of God. Today, as I write this, I recall some fifty years or so ago, at a job fair, I was told that if I went into the ministry, it would be a "fairly easy" way to make a living. I was already preaching at the time and remember thinking this person didn't know what they were talking about.

The purpose of the church has many aspects:

1. To get people saved
2. To teach the gospel, the truth of God's Word to believers

3. And encourage them to study the Word at home, to know what the Word says

If you know the Word, it's much harder for the disciples of the devil to lead you astray. The devil is continuing to bring things along that look great at the start but end up destroying souls. Preachers are so eager to try to make their churches grow that they grab at all sorts of things, never thinking of the end results. Don't be caught up in the devil's snare; **just because everybody else is doing it doesn't make it right**. Churches too many times are like sheep, but they are following the wrong shepherd, shepherds who are leading them astray.

This idea that churches must change to meet the needs of the people is wrong. **God does not change; people need to change to line up with God's Word.** Churches in their efforts to try to please the people never stop and look at the long-term effect this change will have on the church. Church, stay in the Word of God.

1 John 3:16-17

[16] Hereby perceive we the love of God, because he laid down his life for us: and we ought to lay down our lives for the brethren.
[17] But whoso hath this world's good, and seeth his brother have need, and shutteth up his bowels of compassion from him, how dwelleth the love of God in him?

What's the true test of Christian love? Christian love is doing what's good and not doing that which is evil. Christ laid down his life for us. That's the true test of His love. John states that **we** should love the "brethren" enough that, if need be, we would lay down our lives for the brotherhood. We can relate it to giving blood. Why do we give blood at the blood donor centers? Because it's the right thing to do. By donating blood, we are giving the gift of life to someone in need. I often think, as I am giving blood, who is it going to, and what's their soul's condition, and I pray, Lord if they aren't saved, please give them one more chance. Lord, have compassion on them; do not let them be lost. Jesus died for the lost, of which I was one. But now I can truly say, "I once was lost, I once was a sinner, but today I am saved by the grace of God." Jesus' blood covers a multitude of sins.

Romans 5:6-10

> *⁶ For when we were yet without strength, in due time Christ died for the ungodly.*
> *⁷ For scarcely for a righteous man will one die: yet peradventure for a good man some would even dare to die.*
> *⁸ But God commendeth his love toward us, in that, while we were yet sinners, Christ died for us.*
> *⁹ Much more then, being now justified by his blood, we shall be saved from wrath through him.*
> *¹⁰ For if, when we were enemies, we were reconciled to God by the death of his Son, much more, being reconciled, we shall be saved by his life.*

Jesus hasn't asked us to lay down our lives, at least not yet. However, **the Word does ask us to help our brothers in need**. Don't be like Cain and ask, "Am I my brother's keeper?" Show forth that Christ-like love to the lost. There are many people in this world who just need a friend, to know that someone cares about them. Part of these people are in the church. Let them know we're there for them. We'll be surprised how much it will change them and help them.

The sooner we learn that we are not in this battle alone, the better off we will be. This is why we must stress fellowship among the brethren. When we feel that no one cares, that we're all alone, we get to the place where we question if there's any use in going on. We can be assured that the devil is telling us to go ahead and quit. It's a lonely place to be in. But when we find that we're not alone, that there are others who care and serve God, and that they want to be friends and help, life seems so much better.

1 John 3:18

My little children, let us not love in word, neither in tongue; but in deed and in truth.

The essence of true Christian love is to not love in words but rather to love in deeds, helping and encouraging each other in the Lord to share the experience of serving the Lord. **People are tired of fakes who say one thing and do another.** Sadly, the church is full of such people, people who put on a good show, but that's all it is, a good show. Today people want something that's real. There's an old saying, and it's very true. "You don't really know who your friends are until you're in need." True love and friendship will be there in the time of need. Fair weather friends are of very little use to anyone. Be true, be faithful and God will bless you beyond measure. **It's time to do something for God**, to say, like Paul, "Lord, what will thou have me to do?" Pray, find God's will for your life and do it.

Matthew 25:31-46

31 When the Son of man shall come in his glory, and all the holy angels with him, then shall he sit upon the throne of his glory:

32 And before him shall be gathered all nations: and he shall separate them one from another, as a shepherd divideth his sheep from the goats:

33 And he shall set the sheep on his right hand, but the goats on the left.

34 Then shall the King say unto them on his right hand, Come, ye blessed of my Father, inherit the kingdom prepared for you from the foundation of the world:

35 For I was an hungred, and ye gave me meat: I was thirsty, and ye gave me drink: I was a stranger, and ye took me in:

36 Naked, and ye clothed me: I was sick, and ye visited me: I was in prison, and ye came unto me.

37 Then shall the righteous answer him, saying, Lord, when saw we thee an hungred, and fed thee? or thirsty, and gave thee drink?

38 When saw we thee a stranger, and took thee in? or naked, and clothed thee?

39 Or when saw we thee sick, or in prison, and came unto thee?

40 And the King shall answer and say unto them, Verily I say unto you, Inasmuch as ye have done it unto one of the least of these my brethren, ye have done it unto me.

41 Then shall he say also unto them on the left hand, Depart from me, ye cursed, into everlasting fire, prepared for the devil and his angels:

⁴² For I was an hungred, and ye gave me no meat: I was thirsty, and ye gave me no drink:

⁴³ I was a stranger, and ye took me not in: naked, and ye clothed me not: sick, and in prison, and ye visited me not.

⁴⁴ Then shall they also answer him, saying, Lord, when saw we thee an hungred, or athirst, or a stranger, or naked, or sick, or in prison, and did not minister unto thee?

⁴⁵ Then shall he answer them, saying, Verily I say unto you, Inasmuch as ye did it not to one of the least of these, ye did it not to me.

⁴⁶ And these shall go away into everlasting punishment: but the righteous into life eternal.

I don't know about you, but I want to be on the Lord's right hand, and I want to go into the blessings of the Lord. How about you?

1 John 3:19-22

¹⁹ And hereby we know that we are of the truth, and shall assure our hearts before him.

²⁰ For if our heart condemn us, God is greater than our heart, and knoweth all things.

²¹ Beloved, if our heart condemn us not, then have we confidence toward God.

²² And whatsoever we ask, we receive of him, because we keep his commandments, and do those things that are pleasing in his sight.

John, in these verses, talks about the heart. The heart is the center of our being. When we accept Christ as our Savior, we say that Jesus comes into our heart to live. Our heart is the home of the soul; **sin affects the heart because that's where the soul abides**. I've had people tell me that the mind is where the soul is, but I disagree. Yes, I know that scripture speaks of the renewing of our minds. However, the heart is the center of our emotions, for from the heart, the mouth speaks. We pray for a new heart at salvation, not a new mind. We want a heart that's tender to the voice of God, a heart that feels compassion.

When you met your spouse, did they steal your heart or your mind? Love comes from the heart. The mind doesn't love; it reasons. It thinks, but it doesn't love. The heart loves with a tender and compassionate love. The love of Christ toward us is tender and true. The love we give through Christ to others is just as tender, compassionate and true. Why? Because **the spirit of Jesus Christ lives within our hearts**. John, in these verses, gives us a threefold look at our hearts.

In Verse 19, we look at a confirming heart. John said that we can know that we are of the truth, because our hearts are assured before God. We can know that we know we are saved, born again and on our way to heaven. **The spirit will bear witness with our spirit that all is well with our soul**, for by grace are we saved.

Verse 20 speaks of a condemning heart. Before we were saved, our hearts condemned us because of sin. We found ourselves guilty before God for all of our ungodly acts. Just before salvation, our condemning heart brought God's conviction before us, making us realize just how sinful we really were, teaching us that salvation was the only answer to our dilemma, and that things had to change, or we would be lost forever. Jesus was the answer, and he was our only hope. **Jesus came in, and out went all the anger, bitterness, pride, lust and resentment.** Jesus took it all away. The devil tries to bring it back at times, but as 1 John 4:4

states: "*. . . because greater is He that is in me than he that is in the world.*" Jesus gives us joy for sadness. He gives peace and contentment and takes away sorrow and pain.

Verse 21 tells us that we can have a confident heart. When we can feel the power of God, we can come before Him confident in our heart that God will accept us and that there will be no rejection. Some professing Christians say they don't know whether they are saved or not and won't know until they stand before God. We can have a know-so salvation. If I didn't know whether I was saved or not, I'd be finding out. If you don't know for sure about your salvation, I say you're not saved and need to make yourself an altar somewhere and make things right with God.

In Verse 22 we learn that with a just and true heart, we can go before God, and in his presence, we can worship him, praise Him and give glory to Him, knowing that there's nothing that stands between us and God. When we begin to pray, one of the very first things that we must do is examine ourselves in the light of God. It's important to make sure there's nothing that will hinder our talk with the Lord. Then we can begin to give praise and thanksgiving to the Lord and give honor to whom honor is due, Jesus Christ our Savior and Lord. **It's important to enter his presence with praise** for all that He's done for us and worship because we know how much He loves us and the price that He paid, so that we who are unworthy could come into fellowship with Him. We are blessed beyond measure.

How do you think God feels when He sees how people act today? Scripture tells us that in the days of Noah, God repented that He had ever made man. But in all the sin and woes, one man found grace in the eyes of the Lord. One man changed the mind of God. God told Noah what to do to save himself and his family. God is a just God.

Genesis 6:8-18

8 But Noah found grace in the eyes of the LORD.

9 These are the generations of Noah: Noah was a just man and perfect in his generations, and Noah walked with God.

10 And Noah begat three sons, Shem, Ham, and Japheth.

11 The earth also was corrupt before God, and the earth was filled with violence.

12 And God looked upon the earth, and, behold, it was corrupt; for all flesh had corrupted his way upon the earth.

13 And God said unto Noah, The end of all flesh is come before me; for the earth is filled with violence through them; and, behold, I will destroy them with the earth.

14 Make thee an ark of gopher wood; rooms shalt thou make in the ark, and shalt pitch it within and without with pitch.

15 And this is the fashion which thou shalt make it of: The length of the ark shall be three hundred cubits, the breadth of it fifty cubits, and the height of it thirty cubits.

16 A window shalt thou make to the ark, and in a cubit shalt thou finish it above; and the door of the ark shalt thou set in the side thereof; with lower, second, and third stories shalt thou make it.

17 And, behold, I, even I, do bring a flood of waters upon the earth, to destroy all flesh, wherein is the breath of life, from under heaven; and every thing that is in the earth shall die.

18 But with thee will I establish my covenant; and thou shalt come into the ark, thou, and thy sons, and thy wife, and thy sons' wives with thee.

Sometimes we can be so unthankful before God, when we need to just look around us at all He's done. When we come before God, **we need to come in humbleness**, making our needs and petitions known unto Him. Some say that God knows what we have need of even before we ask, so why should we have to ask? One of our common faults is ignorance, ignorance toward God as well as other things. I know that I'm blessed, and **I feel humble to know what my salvation cost**. How much I'm loved! Praise Him, worship Him, give Him glory.

1 John 3:23-24

[23] And this is his commandment, That we should believe on the name of his Son Jesus Christ, and love one another, as he gave us commandment.
[24] And he that keepeth his commandments dwelleth in him, and he in him. And hereby we know that he abideth in us, by the Spirit which he hath given us.

John Phillips writes: "God makes no bones about it. He commands people to believe on the name of His Son, the name that is above every name, the name before which every knee will bow and which every tongue will one day confess (Phil. 2:10-11). God commands all men everywhere to pay homage to that name.

"This commandment was given in the Upper Room, and John was there when it was given. As the Lord passed on to His disciples the great truths He had received from His Father (John 14:13-15, 15:12-16, 17:14), so John now passes them on in his turn. God is very jealous of the name of His Son. That name is honored in heaven but too often is dishonored on earth."

To the Christian, the true child of God, we know that believing on the name of the Lord Jesus Christ is the only way to salvation. To be saved we must believe that Jesus is God's only Son and that **there is salvation in no other name** but the name of Jesus.

Acts 4:10-12

[10] Be it known unto you all, and to all the people of Israel, that by the name of Jesus Christ of Nazareth, whom ye crucified, whom God raised from the dead, even by him doth this man stand here before you whole.
[11] This is the stone which was set at nought of you builders, which is become the head of the corner.
[12] Neither is there salvation in any other: for there is none other name under heaven given among men, whereby we must be saved.

There's a relatively new universal doctrine that's making its way into the church. This doctrine states that everyone is saved. All we must do is be true to our conscience, and we'll all go to heaven. This doctrine sounds good. Under it we don't have any do's and don't's. The only problem is that its origin springs straight out of hell. Nevertheless, preachers and teachers out of the false dictates of their worldly hearts are running after it as hard as they can.

Why, you ask? Because these false preachers and teachers know that if people don't have to change their way of life or their way of living, they will jump on the bandwagon calling themselves Christian, but **they are Christians in name only**. They've never met the Master. There's power in the name of Jesus, power to save, power to heal, power to walk the straight and narrow, and power to be called the sons of God. However, **there has to be a change**, an inward change.

Matthew 7:13-14

> *¹³ Enter ye in at the strait gate: for wide is the gate, and broad is the way, that leadeth to destruction, and many there be which go in thereat:*
> *¹⁴ Because strait is the gate, and narrow is the way, which leadeth unto life, and few there be that find it.*

It's easy to say, "I'm a Christian," but **it's another thing to live a Christian life before God**. It's like the song *Guilty of Love* states: Guilty of love in the first degree. If you were brought to court for being a Christian, would there be enough evidence to convict you? Think about it. Do we love one another as Christ commands; or **are we all mouth and no action?** Just where do we really stand? Only you know the answer to that, so I ask you one more time to think about it.

One Bible scholar spoke of a mystical relationship between Christ and man, but I see nothing mystical about it. As scripture puts it, it's simple: "For God so loved the world."

John 3:14-17

> *¹⁴ And as Moses lifted up the serpent in the wilderness, even so must the Son of man be lifted up:*
> *¹⁵ That whosoever believeth in him should not perish, but have eternal life.*
> *¹⁶ For God so loved the world, that he gave his only begotten Son, that whosoever believeth in him should not per-*

142

ish, but have everlasting life.

[17] For God sent not his Son into the world to condemn the world; but that the world through him might be saved.

In the very beginning, God made us to look like Him. Why? **So that there could be friendship, companionship and fellowship with God.** And, yes, the world thinks we're crazy, but who cares, as long as God loves us.

Genesis 3:8

And they heard the voice of the LORD God walking in the garden in the cool of the day: and Adam and his wife hid themselves from the presence of the LORD God amongst the trees of the garden.

Genesis 5:21-24

[21] And Enoch lived sixty and five years, and begat Methuselah:

[22] And Enoch walked with God after he begat Methuselah three hundred years, and begat sons and daughters:

[23] And all the days of Enoch were three hundred sixty and five years:

[24] And Enoch walked with God: and he was not; for God took him.

Genesis 6:9

These are the generations of Noah: Noah was a just man and perfect in his generations, and Noah walked with God.

We can walk with God daily. He may not come to earth and walk with us as in Genesis, but he does even better. He comes and lives in our heart twenty-four hours a day. He never leaves us nor forsakes us; he is always there just a thought away. We don't have to go to a temple to find God, because our bodies are the temple. We don't have to go to a priest, because, according to the Word, we are priests before God. God, through Jesus' sacrifice on the cross, has made everything open to us. **There's no longer a vail to separate us from God**; the vail is gone, and everything has been done so that we can have direct access to the throne room of God. If we are lost for all eternity, we can't blame God. He'll not make us serve Him. That decision we must make on our own. **Will you be lost or saved? You decide.**

Chapter 3 – Test Your Knowledge

1. What does Verse 1 tell us about?

_____

_____

_____

2. After we have been saved we become the

_____

_____

3. There are three ways to become a member of a family.

What are they?

_____

_____

_____

4. Who makes up the bride of Christ?

_____

_____

_____

5. Is it possible to live a perfect life in the sight of God?

_____

6. When was the law of Moses done away with?

_____

_____

7. Are the Ten Commandments still to be followed?

_____

8. The law was given to define what?

_____

_____

9. God will not force us to serve Him and what is it that Satan cannot force us to do?

_____

_____

10. Sin is basically a matter of

_____

11. Is it possible to be obedient on the outside while rebelling on the inside? _____

12. What goes before a fall?

_____

13. If you are a practitioner of sin you are not

_____

14. The body is only a vessel; who has control over it?

_____

15. Love does not separate the children of God, instead it does what?

_____

_____

16. The ministry is not a life of ease, what type of life is it?

_____

_____

17. Cain killed his brother. What was his brother's name?

_____

18. The essence of true Christian love is not to love in words but what?

_____

19. Who found grace in the eyes of the Lord?

_____

20. What is going to happen at the name of Jesus?

_____

_____

_____

Chapter 4

1 John 4:1-3

¹ Beloved, believe not every spirit, but try the spirits whether they are of God: because many false prophets are gone out into the world.
² Hereby know ye the Spirit of God: Every spirit that confesseth that Jesus Christ is come in the flesh is of God:
³ And every spirit that confesseth not that Jesus Christ is come in the flesh is not of God: and this is that spirit of antichrist, whereof ye have heard that it should come; and even now already is it in the world.

One more time, John comes back to the same point in this fourth chapter. That point is love, for **if we love one another, we are of Christ**. Here we need to look at this chapter a little differently. John starts out by telling us not to believe every spirit, but that we are to try the spirits to see if they are of God. Furthermore, John speaks of false prophets who are gone out into the world. Times have changed since John's day. The persecutions the church faced then have changed, but **the devil is still the enemy of God and His church**. When people walk through the church doors, there's only one way to tell if they're friend or foe. There's

149

so much falsehood in the church today that we cannot afford to accept what people say.

We must rely on the Holy Ghost for the answer. Do our spirits bear witness one with another? There are nine gifts of the Holy Ghost, and we need to look at one of them: discernment. The discerning of spirits is one of the three gifts of revelation.

1 Corinthians 12:1-4

¹ Now concerning spiritual gifts, brethren, I would not have you ignorant.

² Ye know that ye were Gentiles, carried away unto these dumb idols, even as ye were led.

³ Wherefore I give you to understand, that no man speaking by the Spirit of God calleth Jesus accursed: and that no man can say that Jesus is the Lord, but by the Holy Ghost.

⁴ Now there are diversities of gifts, but the same Spirit.

To provide some background, there are nine gifts of the Holy Ghost; they can be broken into three groups. The first of these is the group of revelation. The gifts of revelation are gifts where God reveals to us what He wants us to know, when He wants us to know it.

First are the gifts of Revelation:

The gift of Wisdom
The gift of the Word of Knowledge
The gift of Discerning of Spirits

Second are the gifts of Power:

> The gift of Faith
> The gift of Miracles
> The gift of Healing

Third are the gifts of Utterance:

> The gift of Prophecy
> The gift of Tongues
> The gift of Interpretation of Tongues

These gifts need to be working in the church today; sadly, most of them are not. The gift we'll focus on now is the Discerning of Spirits. To quote from my book, *A Study on the Holy Ghost,* we can see **just how important it is to have this discerning of spirits**; without it, how can we try the spirits?

"Discerning of Spirits is such an important phase of spiritual knowledge, that it is honored with recognition apart from the gift of the Word of Knowledge. The reason for this lies in the value which this gift has in Christian life and ministry.

"There are two realms of the spirit world. The great-unseen world of spirits is divided into the good and evil. Our Lord God and Satan are the rulers over these respective realms. Cherubim, seraphim and angels do the bidding of God. Principalities, powers and rulers of the darkness of this world, wicked spirits in high places, and evil spirits and demons are all under the authority of Satan. These two realms are arrayed against each other, and the war of the ages is still going on. The Holy Ghost is the active Commander-in-Chief of God's army. He personally indwells and energizes spirit-filled believers. Discerning of spirits is a valuable weapon both of defense and offense for the spirit-filled believer.

"In the realm of affliction, the Bible speaks of dumb spirits (Matthew 9:21); blind spirits (Matthew 12:22); deaf spirits (Matthew 9:25); spirits of infirmity (Luke 13:11, 16); and spirits of lunacy (Matthew 14:15, 18). There are also cases of those who were just 'possessed with devils' (Matthew 4:24).

"The gift of discerning of spirits enables the saints of God to approach these cases with knowledge and understanding. With the word of authority, he cast out the evil spirits (Mark 16:17). Paul's reference to seducing spirits and doctrines of devils (1 Timothy 4:1) reveals a very subtle trick of Satan to deceive mankind. Also, in the last days will come false prophets, who will perform miracles with signs and lying wonders in the name of the antichrist (2 Thessalonians 2:9 and Revelations 13:14).

"Without the gift of discerning of spirits or discernment, we would not recognize these evil spirits that surrounds us. They dwell on every hand and can only be recognized through the gift of discernment. The Word tells us to know those that labor among us; this can only be done as God reveals to us their true spiritual nature. Not everyone that is evil is possessed of evil spirits, but a good many are. We must be open to the voice of God as He speaks to us concerning those evil spirits. Every spirit-filled believer needs the gift of discernment to fulfill God's calling in his or her life."

In our world, there's so much lying that we hardly know who to believe and who not to. So, we must rely on God and His spiritual gifts. John says to try the spirits to see if they be of God. It's sad that God isn't welcome in most churches, and falsehood is taking over in what was once the true church world. **Preachers and teachers no longer want to preach and teach the truth.** It's like everybody is afraid that they might be criticized or persecuted for telling the truth of God's Word. If the Bible, God's Holy Word, says that certain things are sin, **then they are sin**.

It might make the sinner feel better when preachers won't preach and teach on sin, but look at it this way: The preachers and Christians say they love you, but do they really? The Christian who loves you will try to warn you about sin and where that sin will cause you to spend eternity. The people who really don't love you or care about you won't take the time to warn you about sin and where your soul will spend eternity. So, who loves you the most? The preachers who preach on sin, or the preachers who refuse to preach on sin?

It's better to have someone who cares enough to tell us about the consequences of sin and where we will spend eternity. The spirit of the antichrist is in the world today, and it's even in the church. Christians, pray for the church, for the power of God to fill it one more time. When sinners come to church and feel comfortable sitting in the pews, something is very wrong.

1 John 4:4-6

⁴ Ye are of God, little children, and have overcome them: because greater is he that is in you, than he that is in the world.
⁵ They are of the world: therefore speak they of the world, and the world heareth them.
⁶ We are of God: he that knoweth God heareth us; he that is not of God heareth not us. Hereby know we the spirit of truth, and the spirit of error.

Verse 4 begins by John telling the church that they were of God and not to believe the lies of the devil. They were to always claim the blessings and promises of God, **because as His children, the blessings were theirs to claim**. The God they served was greater than anything the devil could throw at them. As scripture states it, ". . . *because greater is he that is in you, than he that is in the world.*" (1 John 4:4) We are made overcomers by the word of our testimony and by the blood of the Lamb.

Revelation 12:11

> *And they overcame him by the blood of the Lamb, and by the word of their testimony; and they loved not their lives unto the death.*

This epistle shows us three secrets of overcoming power:

> The Word of God abides in you.
> The seed of God abides in you.
> God Himself abides in you.

The precious Word of God gives us strength; the Word is power to the child of God. The Word of God is as a sharp, two-edged sword with which to fight the enemy. Remember, **Jesus is the Word**. Scripture says that the Word was with God, and the Word was God. The Word is a lamp unto our feet and a light unto our path. As we read and study the Word of God, we renew that power to believe God will do just what He said He'll do. We need to renew our minds daily with God's Word; keeping it fresh and powerful, and in a moment's notice, have it readily at hand to fight the devil. **Ignorance of God's Word is the church's worst enemy.** Without knowledge of God's Word, we are prey for the devil and his demons. The Word of God is a sharp, two-edged sword with which we can put the devil to flight.

Ephesians 6:17

> *And take the helmet of salvation, and the sword of the Spirit, which is the Word of God:*

Hebrews 4:12

> *For the Word of God is quick, and powerful, and sharper than any twoedged sword, piercing even to the dividing asunder of soul and spirit, and of the joints and marrow, and is a discerner of the thoughts and intents of the heart.*

God gives us everything we need to live for Him and do His work. Whither we realize it or not, we bear, or carry, the seeds of God within us. It's the gospel seed; the seed we sow every time we witness to the lost or pass out gospel tracts. Each time we tell our friends about our church and invite them to come to church with us, that precious seed springs forth to the glory of God. The seed is the gospel message, the story of Jesus and what He can do for us.

The third secret is that Jesus Christ abides within us. Every moment of every day, Jesus is with us, because His divine spirit lives within the heart of every true believer.

Romans 8:9-11

> [9] *But ye are not in the flesh, but in the Spirit, if so be that the Spirit of God dwell in you. Now if any man have not the Spirit of Christ, he is none of his.*

¹⁰ And if Christ be in you, the body is dead because of sin; but the Spirit is life because of righteousness.

¹¹ But if the Spirit of him that raised up Jesus from the dead dwell in you, he that raised up Christ from the dead shall also quicken your mortal bodies by his Spirit that dwelleth in you.

2 Corinthians 6:16

And what agreement hath the temple of God with idols? for ye are the temple of the living God; as God hath said, I will dwell in them, and walk in them; and I will be their God, and they shall be my people.

Ephesians 3:17

That Christ may dwell in your hearts by faith; that ye, being rooted and grounded in love,

This body is the temple of the living God; He lives within us twenty-four hours a day. The only thing that will cause Jesus to leave us, to leave this temple, is if we give over to sin. It's not popular to preach that a person can backslide and go to hell, but the Word of God shows us it can happen. I know that I'm saved by grace and not by works, for by grace are ye saved, this I know and believe. Nevertheless, **we can turn our back on that grace and walk away from it, back to the world of sin**.

There are some that say that if you believe a person can be saved and then lose their salvation, then you don't believe in the working of grace. The following passages from the Bible tell us differently.

Galatians 5:4

Christ is become of no effect unto you, whosoever of you are justified by the law; ye are fallen from grace.

Matthew 7:21-23

[21] Not every one that saith unto me, Lord, Lord, shall enter into the kingdom of heaven; but he that doeth the will of my Father which is in heaven.
[22] Many will say to me in that day, Lord, Lord, have we not prophesied in thy name? and in thy name have cast out devils? and in thy name done many wonderful works?
[23] And then will I profess unto them, I never knew you: depart from me, ye that work iniquity.

1 Timothy 4:1-2

[1] Now the Spirit speaketh expressly, that in the latter times some shall depart from the faith, giving heed to seducing spirits, and doctrines of devils;
[2] Speaking lies in hypocrisy; having their conscience seared with a hot iron;

Ezekiel 18:24

But when the righteous turneth away from his righteousness, and committeth iniquity, and doeth according to all the abominations that the wicked man doeth, shall he live?

All his righteousness that he hath done shall not be mentioned: in his trespass that he hath trespassed, and in his sin that he hath sinned, in them shall he die.

I believe in God's saving grace, but **grace doesn't and never will give a person a free pass to sin and transgress God's law**. To believe this is to be devoid of good sense. The old nature that condemned us to hell before we were saved, if given the chance to rise up again, will once again condemn us to a devil's hell. Read the Word, for **in the Word there is life through Jesus Christ our Lord**. Please don't take man's word for anything until you check it for yourself. We are too near the end of this race; don't let someone turn you aside now. Read the Word, try the spirits and trust God to show you the way. Find a place where the Word is preached, the true Word of God.

Remember that the spirit of the antichrist is already in the world today. The devil is preparing the world for the great antichrist to come and rule the world. This antichrist will be a very real man; he's been called by many names: the man of sin, the son of perdition and the beast. He's all of these. His coming has been foretold over and over by the men of God. Satan's false christ will come to power, make no mistake about it. **The only thing that has held the devil in check until now is the power of God and the Holy Ghost, the defender of the church.** The antichrist spirit is working hard to get everything just right for the antichrist to assume power. End time deceptions are overwhelming the world. We see the great falling away taking place now, today, in this very hour. The end time war between good and evil has been raging for over two thousand years. The devil thinks he's winning, but the battle belongs to Christ Jesus our Lord.

1 John 4:7-8

⁷ Beloved, let us love one another: for love is of God; and every one that loveth is born of God, and knoweth God. ⁸ He that loveth not knoweth not God; for God is love.

John expresses God in three ways:

> **1. God is a spirit** – (John 4:24) *God is a Spirit: and they that worship him must worship him in spirit and in truth.*

> **2. God is light and this light is the light of our souls that dispels the darkness** – (John 1:1-5) *¹ In the beginning was the Word, and the Word was with God, and the Word was God. ² The same was in the beginning with God. ³ All things were made by him; and without him was not any thing made that was made. ⁴ In him was life; and the life was the light of men. ⁵ And the light shineth in darkness; and the darkness comprehended it not.*

> **3. God is love** – (John 3:16) *For God so loved the world, that he gave his only begotten Son, that whosoever believeth in him should not perish, but have everlasting life.* (1 John 4:8, 16) *⁸ He that loveth not knoweth not God; for God is love. ¹⁶ And we have known and believed the love that God hath to us. God is love; and he that dwelleth in love dwelleth in God, and God in him.*

We know these statements only give us a small part of the picture of who God is, but it's a start in trying to comprehend the impossible to understand. We will never understand God, not on this earth or in heaven. But we can have some sense of God's person. I dare say we will never understand God's love for us, or how He was willing to let Jesus come and die that we might have fellowship with Him.

The closest I can think of is a testimony I heard. A young preacher had just taken the pulpit and told the congregation he wanted to tell them a story.

A man took his son and his son's friend sailing. While they were on the ocean, a storm came up, and the small sailboat was tossed about. A large wave hit the boat, and the man's son and his friend were thrown overboard. The man only had time to save one of them. Did he rescue his son who was saved and knew the Lord, or his son's friend who wasn't saved? The man reached out and caught his son's friend. **Why, some might ask, would a father not save his son first?** The young man asked his friend's father why he didn't save his son and let him drown. The man replied that his son was saved and ready to meet the Lord, while his son's friend wasn't saved and wasn't ready.

The young preacher told the congregation he was the boy that was saved, and their pastor was the man who reached out and saved him. **Because of their pastor's love for the lost, he was there to minister to them.** Their pastor would see his son again in heaven, and so would he.

This is the Father's love for us. How great a love!

What do we really know about God? God is a spirit person. He has a body, whether spirit or flesh. We are made in His image or likeness. He has feet and legs, He walked in the garden with Adam and Eve in the cool of the evenings. He walked and talked with Enoch and also with Noah. He has arms and hands, for, *"His arm is not short that He cannot save."* He has eyes and ears and a mouth, for he hears and speaks if we will take the time to listen. We are wonderfully and fearfully made in the likeness, in the image of God.

Wiersbe says this about God: "God is love. This does not mean that 'love is God.' And the fact that two people love each other does not mean that their love is necessarily holy. It has accurately been said that 'love does not define God, but God defines love.' God is love and God is light; therefore, His love is a holy love, and His holiness is expressed in love. All that God does expresses all that God is. Even His judgements are measured out in love and mercy (Lam. 3:22-23)."

1 John 4:9-11

⁹ In this was manifested the love of God toward us, because that God sent his only begotten Son into the world, that we might live through him.
¹⁰ Herein is love, not that we loved God, but that he loved us, and sent his Son to be the propitiation for our sins.
¹¹ Beloved, if God so loved us, we ought also to love one another.

God's love was brought out into the open for all to see when He sent Jesus His only begotten Son into this world to prepare the way for man's salvation. Man was under the rule of the law, but **the law couldn't do what was needed to bring man into divine fellowship with God**. There had to be one supreme sacrifice, a sacrifice that was special enough to do what the blood of animals couldn't. Did God know that man would fall in the garden? I believe the answer is yes, He did.

God is all-knowing, and I believe that the creation of man was weighed in the balances before man was ever created. The price for man's salvation was also taken into account and deemed worth the cost. Why? Because down through the thousands of years, there would be countless numbers who would give themselves over to God and His service. These multiplied millions or billions served God out of love for all He's done for them, because Jesus laid down His life that we might be saved from sin and hell.

Those who accept the Biblical story of Jesus on the cross, not being believers, believe that the Romans took Jesus' life and that Jesus could do nothing about it. We who have had a personal experience with Christ know the truth; **Jesus gave His life as a ransom for us**. What the devil doesn't like, he tries to explain away. Men and women who are acclaimed Bible scholars have tried to explain away every miracle in the Bible. They've tried to do away with the power and authority of God and bring God down to man's level.

However, if they are so smart and know all about God's Word, then they surely know they will burn in the very hell they say does not exist. It seems strange that a person can be so educated and so ignorant at the same time. The answer is this, **when you're a Christian in name only, you don't believe in the true power of God**. This is what's happening today across this world; churches that are supposed to believe God's Word and stand on it are changing. They are holding their conventions and conferences and talking about what the Bibles says, then, instead of standing up for God's truth, they bow their heads and in shame give in to the pressure of the world. They change their church doctrines to conform to Satan's will. Where these churches in the past preached against sin and moral decay, preached the truth and saw souls saved and born again; they will from now on preach a perverted gospel, a gospel that has no power or truth, that cannot bring conviction and that surely cannot save the lost.

What does all of this mean? It means that the church no longer loves the sinner; the church no longer has compassion for the lost. **The church has become a business.** Their aim is to take people's money, to make them feel good in their sins and to lull them to sleep spiritually. No matter how they live or what they do, everybody is going to heaven. This is called universalism, and it's a lie straight from the very pit of hell. A preacher who won't preach the truth of God's Word is a thief, because he's stealing the Word of God from you. He's a coward, because he's afraid he might make you mad. He's a liar, because he won't tell you the truth. He's a blind leader of the blind, and they both will fall into hell together.

1 Timothy 4:1-4

[1] Now the Spirit speaketh expressly, that in the latter times some shall depart from the faith, giving heed to seducing spirits, and doctrines of devils;
[2] Speaking lies in hypocrisy; having their conscience seared with a hot iron;
[3] Forbidding to marry, and commanding to abstain from meats, which God hath created to be received with thanksgiving of them which believe and know the truth.
[4] For every creature of God is good, and nothing to be refused, if it be received with thanksgiving:

Matthew 15:13-14

[13] But he answered and said, Every plant, which my heavenly Father hath not planted, shall be rooted up.

¹⁴ Let them alone: they be blind leaders of the blind. And if the blind lead the blind, both shall fall into the ditch.

Luke 6:39

And he spake a parable unto them, Can the blind lead the blind? shall they not both fall into the ditch?

2 Timothy 3:1-5

¹ This know also, that in the last days perilous times shall come.

² For men shall be lovers of their own selves, covetous, boasters, proud, blasphemers, disobedient to parents, unthankful, unholy,

³ Without natural affection, trucebreakers, false accusers, incontinent, fierce, despisers of those that are good,

⁴ Traitors, heady, highminded, lovers of pleasures more than lovers of God;

⁵ Having a form of godliness, but denying the power thereof: from such turn away.

2 Thessalonians 2:9-12

⁹ Even him, whose coming is after the working of Satan with all power and signs and lying wonders,

¹⁰ And with all deceivableness of unrighteousness in them that perish; because they received not the love of the truth, that they might be saved.

¹¹ And for this cause God shall send them strong delusion, that they should believe a lie:

12 That they all might be damned who believed not the truth, but had pleasure in unrighteousness.

We have very little time left before Jesus comes in the rapture (the catching away). The devil is working overtime to drag down as many as possible. We must pray as never before for the lost. Jesus has paid the price for the souls of man. Now the question is, **what are we going to do about what's going on in the world today?** It's time that we begin to stay on our knees before God. If the church will bind together and pray, we can change things. *"The effectual fervent prayer of a righteous man availeth much."*

James 5:13-16

13 Is any among you afflicted? let him pray. Is any merry? let him sing psalms.
14 Is any sick among you? let him call for the elders of the church; and let them pray over him, anointing him with oil in the name of the Lord:
15 And the prayer of faith shall save the sick, and the Lord shall raise him up; and if he have committed sins, they shall be forgiven him.
16 Confess your faults one to another, and pray one for another, that ye may be healed. The effectual fervent prayer of a righteous man availeth much.

Prayer is our lifeline to God. When we cease to pray, we become cold and indifferent in our souls. Then it won't be long before we completely backslide. This is why we stress over and over that a child of God must pray. We've all seen shows of divers going down deep in the sea; they put on their diving suit with its air line; that air line is their lifeline. Cut the air off, and they'll die. Prayer is our lifeline; **stop the prayer, and we'll spiritually die**. It's not God's desire that we spiritually die, but it is the devil's. Do you spiritually live or die? Only you can make that decision. No one can make it for you.

In Jesus Christ, there is love, love for God, love for our fellow Christians and love and compassion for the souls of lost men and women. There's only one thing that a child of God can hate, and that's sin. Here's where a lot of people get confused. **We hate the sin, but we must love the sinner**; and they are two different things.

Prostitutes who sell their bodies, we are to love them with a Christ-like love while at the same time hating their lifestyle and their sin. Let's look at ourselves: God loved us while we were yet sinners; He hated our sin, but He loved us. **We must learn to separate the sinner from their sin.** We must have a true, God-given love for the lost souls of sinners, while hating the sinful lifestyle they live. This is the true love of Jesus Christ that's shed abroad to a sinful world.

1 John 4:12-16

[12] No man hath seen God at any time. If we love one an-other, God dwelleth in us, and his love is perfected in us.
[13] Hereby know we that we dwell in him, and he in us, be-cause he hath given us of his Spirit.
[14] And we have seen and do testify that the Father sent the Son to be the Saviour of the world. [15] Whosoever shall confess that Jesus is the Son of God, God dwelleth in him, and he in God.

¹⁶ And we have known and believed the love that God hath to us. God is love; and he that dwelleth in love dwelleth in God, and God in him.

John continually talks about love, but the love that John talks about is the love that comes from the heart of true believers; a godly love that looks past all of the sin of this world and sees the souls that are burdened down under a load of sin. This godly love is not the kind of love that a husband has for a wife. It's the love that Jesus has for the lost; it's the love that took Him to the cross, there to lay down His life that we might have life and have it more abundantly. Jesus' love has brought us into the true fellowship with God. Fellowship is vital to a Christian experience with God. **We must be able to talk to Jesus anytime, anyplace, day or night.** This companionship brings us into the very presence of Jesus and God. We don't have to look for someone to go before God for us; **we can go boldly before God ourselves**; this is the love that God gives to us.

Moreover, God indwells His saints; His spirit comes into the hearts of believers. There God begins to work a work, to perfect us in His image. In His likeness, **we are to show the world the living spirit of God**. The world is full of counterfeit Christians; these are Christians in name only. They don't have the spirit of God, but have the spirit of the world. The world knows its own. You see every day those on TV and hear those every day on the radio that claim to be holy and righteous, but there's no truth in them. The world is tired of the fake and the false. Is it any wonder that people don't want to attend church? The world judges the church by what they see and hear on TV and radio.

The Wiersbe Bible Commentary relates this story: "A Salvation Army worker found a derelict woman alone on the street

167

and invited her to come into the chapel for help, but the woman refused to move. The worker assured her, 'We love you and want to help you. God loves you. Jesus died for you.' But the woman did not budge.

"As if on divine impulse, the Army lassie leaned over and kissed the woman on the cheek, taking her into her arms. The woman began to sob, and like a child, was led into the chapel, where she ultimately trusted Christ.

'You told me that God loved me,' she said later, 'but it wasn't till you showed me that God loved me that I wanted to be saved.'" To be effective, **we must show forth the love of Jesus Christ to the world**. It's not enough to say it; the world must be shown.

Another example of God's love through us to the world is found in *John Phillips Commentary*. "Adoniram Judson's is a fascinating story. To begin with, Judson was an out-and-out skeptic, and a brilliant one at that, an admirer of Thomas Paine in an age when the French and English atheists were in vogue. Young Judson was shaken, however, by the terrible death of a much admired, skeptical college friend. The young man died in soul agony and mortal terror of eternity, and Judson happened to be in the next room. Judson didn't know the dying man next door was his admired agnostic friend – he just heard his screams and cries of terror, and his appalling fear of death. The next morning, Judson was shaken to discover the identity of the wretched man next door. Soon after, Judson was saved and his life transformed.

"He went to Burma with his bride and arrived in Rangoon in July 1813. The couple lived in a primitive hut on the swamp just outside the town. It was a dreadful spot – the haunt of wild beasts, a place where the city's filth was dumped, and where the dead were buried.

"They were not wanted, and their gospel was not wanted. They suffered appalling privation and persecutions. On one occasion, Judson, reduced to a skeleton, was driven across the desert, his back bleeding from the lash, his feet burned and blistered by the scorching sand. On another occasion he was imprisoned, and for two long years he was locked in a foul cell and tormented by every cruelty that could suggest itself to his brutal guards. In the meantime, his wife was left destitute and the house stripped of all its furniture. His oldest girl came down with smallpox and his youngest child was threatened with starvation.

"Then a sentence of death was passed upon the missionary. The date was set; the hour drew near. But then Judson was smuggled away, and his wife, now completely abandoned, had no idea where he was or if he was still alive. She herself was scarred and maimed, a living skeleton, shorn of her hair and dressed in rags. Eventually, Judson buried his wife and all his children in that heathen land.

"But souls were saved, Judson lived long enough to greet his first convert, establish a church, see it grow to a hundred members, and to translate the whole Bible into Burmese. Then, after thirty years, he took his first furlough."

Judson's moto was, **"Think much on the love of Christ."**

What causes a man like Judson to do what he did? It's the love of Christ. What causes a young convert to go out and begin to tell people about what God has done for him? It's the love of Christ. We may not be called to go to foreign fields to spread the gospel, but we are called, and our mission field may be our neighborhood. Make no mistake about it, we are called to work for the Lord. We are called to show forth the true love of God and to tell the gospel story, to gain converts to the kingdom of God, true converts, those who truly believe in Jesus Christ as Savior, with true repentance, bearing fruit for the Master.

There are many who profess to be Christians but are not; they are counterfeits of the true Christians. They are Christians in name only. As the Bible states in Jude, they are *"twice dead, plucked up by the roots."* And one day soon there's coming a separating, the true from the false. Which side will you be on?

1 John 4:17-19

[17] Herein is our love made perfect, that we may have boldness in the day of judgment: because as he is, so are we in this world.
[18] There is no fear in love; but perfect love casteth out fear: because fear hath torment. He that feareth is not made perfect in love.
[19] We love him, because he first loved us.

"Herein is our love made perfect, that we may have boldness in the day of judgment." As we look at this scripture, it tells us that **at the great white throne of judgment, the saints of God will have no fear**. Why? Because we, the saints, will have already been judged at the judgment seat of Christ. When we stand before Christ's judgment seat, it will be for a judgment on our lives and works. Remember, our sins have already been forgiven; they were forgiven at the time we repented and asked for forgiveness, and God saved us from sin through the blood of Christ.

Romans 14:10

But why dost thou judge thy brother? or why dost thou set at nought thy brother? for we shall all stand before the judgment seat of Christ.

2 Corinthians 5:10

> *For we must all appear before the judgment seat of Christ;*
> *that every one may receive the things done in his body, ac-*
> *cording to that he hath done, whether it be good or bad.*

In Verse 18, John speaks of *"perfect love casteth out fear."* Does this mean that a child of God is without fear? No. It means that **we, as God's children, have an abiding peace knowing that everything is in God's hands and under His control.** When I had a triple bypass surgery, I had a certain amount of fear. It was a fear of the unknown. I knew they would stop my heart from beating. I guessed I'd be technically dead, since my heart was stopped. This was all unknown to me; there was a fear, but at the same time, there was a peace. I knew that everything was in God's hands, and either way I would come out a winner. If I died, I would go on home to be with Jesus; if I lived, I'd be with my earthly family and continue with God's work.

God had given me peace and a scripture to stand on: 1 John 4:4 says, *". . . greater is he that is in you, than he that is in the world."* This word from God kept going through my mind. Even as I slid onto the operating table, that scripture kept going through my mind. To a child of God whose heart is fixed on Jesus, there's peace. The Christians who were put in the Roman arena feared what was going to happen to them, but there was a peace in their hearts greater than the fear of death. They knew they were going home to be with Jesus.

The Romans couldn't understand the Christians who were willing to die for this man, Jesus. If being a Christian wasn't against the law and punishable by death, many Romans probably would have become Christians. The world today, like the Romans of old, doesn't understand true, born-again Christians. They'll **never understand until they experience salvation for themselves**, and a Christian cannot truly explain what salvation is like. They can try, but how do you describe the feeling of having Jesus cleanse you from sin and how it feels to know that Jesus lives within your heart? The feeling of God blessing you is beyond what language can tell. We're saved by grace, and we live by God's grace, but it's so good to be able to feel the presence and the blessings of God as He touches our heart and soul. **It would be a very drab life to have a religion where we couldn't feel the presence of God.**

We know great things await us on the other side, but the greatest thing to me will be to see Jesus. I have family and friends in heaven, and it will be great to see and visit with them. But I want to see Jesus, the one who loved me enough that He died for me. He died that I might live and spend eternity with Him. There's a chorus I like to sing:

> To be like Jesus, to be like Jesus
> All I ask is to be like Him
> All through life's journey
> From earth to glory
> All I ask is to be like Him.

We know that as the scripture teaches, we are to be Christ-like in our words and our actions. We're to show forth a Christ-like spirit and a Christ-like life before this lost and dying world, so that as the world looks upon us, they do not see us, but they see Jesus through us; that we may be as He is to this lost and dying world, a light that shines in the darkness, a beacon of hope where there is no hope, that we might point souls to the cross of Calvary, that we can say come and meet this friend of mine, calling His name Jesus and sharing that He loves us more than we will ever know. Who do we love? Jesus, because He first loved us. He loved us when we were unlovable, He loved us when there was no reason to love us, and still He loved us. **We fall into terrible things when we lose sight of the cross of Calvary.** To lose sight of the cross is to walk away from God. When we walk away from God, we've lost everything that's of value in our lives. The love of God is the only real thing in this world. Everything else has no value and is only falsehood and lies. Love Jesus, serve Him, live for Him and find that peace that satisfies the soul.

1 John 4:20-21

[20] If a man say, I love God, and hateth his brother, he is a liar: for he that loveth not his brother whom he hath seen, how can he love God whom he hath not seen?
[21] And this commandment have we from him, That he who loveth God love his brother also.

In this twentieth verse, John boils everything down to either love or hate. **If I hate my brother, then I cannot love God.** Love and hate cannot exist together. If hate rules our life, then we cannot truly love with a Christ-like love. We see and hear a lot about people who love their family, but hate the person who lives next door. This type of love is a worldly love, where a person picks and chooses whom they love and hate. This is the only way the world knows, and it's all the devil wants them to know. However, **we know another type of love, a Godly love, the type of love that Jesus has for everyone**. This love looks past all of the sin and sees the lost, confused and trapped souls of men and women. Jesus' greatest desire is to set every ensnared soul free, and He will, if they'll only ask. Jesus won't force us to do anything. He wants to save but won't go where He's not invited. There are some that teach that man isn't a free moral agent, but we are. **It's up to us whether we get saved or not.** Jesus doesn't force us to do anything; if He did, then everyone would be saved.

2 Peter 3:9

> *The Lord is not slack concerning his promise, as some men count slackness; but is longsuffering to us-ward, not willing that any should perish, but that all should come to repentance.*

Salvation is up to us; we must make that decision for ourselves. **God doesn't want mankind to go to a devil's hell**, but being a free moral agent, we choose where we will spend eternity, not God.

John tells us that if we hate our brother whom we see, then how can we say we love God, whom we have not seen. We are saved by the grace of God, but **we live by faith in and through Jesus Christ**. There's one thing we must be very careful of, and that's counterfeit Christians. They put on a good show, but that's all it is, a good show. They are like cotton candy. You have a big fluffy amount on a stick, but when you take a bite, it goes to nothing. Counterfeit Christians do great harm to the church. **The only way to deal with these counterfeits is to preach the Word.**

Preach it straight and preach it hard. Counterfeits are looking for a place where they can get the pastor to compromise the Word and lower the standards they preach; preach the Word, preach it straight. **The true believer will stay, worship and praise God**, and the counterfeit Christians will leave, because their goals cannot be reached.

We must learn to be confident in God, stand up for what we believe in and let the world know that God's Word is forever, established, and they cannot change it. No matter how many times they rewrite the Bible and make their changes, it doesn't change God's Word. All they are doing is bringing a curse upon themselves.

Psalm 119:89

For ever, O LORD, thy word is settled in heaven.

Isaiah 40:8

The grass withereth, the flower fadeth: but the word of our God shall stand for ever.

Matthew 24:35

Heaven and earth shall pass away, but my words shall not pass away.

Revelation 22:18-19

[18] For I testify unto every man that heareth the words of the prophecy of this book, If any man shall add unto these

things, God shall add unto him the plagues that are writ-
ten in this book:

[19] And if any man shall take away from the words of the
book of this prophecy, God shall take away his part out of
the book of life, and out of the holy city, and from the
things which are written in this book.

Stand for Jesus, stand for God's Word, and be confident in God and His word. Love the brotherhood of Christian believers. Lift up your heads, for the hour of our redemption draweth nigh. **Give praise unto the Lord.**

Chapter 4 – Test Your Knowledge

1. In Verse 1 John tells us to do two things. What are they?

_____

_____

2. How many gifts of the spirit are there?

_____

3. Names the three groups of gifts of the spirit.

_____

_____

_____

4. What does the gift of discernment reveal to us?

_____

_____

_____

5. Greater is He that is in you than

_____

_____

6. What are the three secrets of overcoming power?

_____

_____

_____

7. Do you think God knew that Adam and Eve would sin?

_____

8. When you are a Christian in name only, you do not believe

in the true _____

9. God indwells the hearts of his

_____

10. Name one attribute of a counterfeit Christian.

_____

11. The saints will have no fear at the great white throne of

judgment. Why? _____

_____

_____

12. Perfect love casts out

_____

13. The feeling of God blessing you is beyond

_____

14. When a man says that he loves God and hates his brother, he is a _____

15. Man was created as a free moral

_____

16. Who decides where we spend eternity?

_____

17. We are saved by the grace of God but we live by

_____

18. What is the only way to deal with a counterfeit Christian?

_____

_____

19. We must learn to be _____

in God.

Chapter 5

1 John 5:1-3

¹ Whosoever believeth that Jesus is the Christ is born of God: and every one that loveth him that begat loveth him also that is begotten of him.
² By this we know that we love the children of God, when we love God, and keep his commandments.
³ For this is the love of God, that we keep his commandments: and his commandments are not grievous.

As we look at this fifth chapter, it seems these first three verses are out of place, that they should have been the last three verses of Chapter 4. This is what most Bible scholars believe, but **God had them put right where He wanted them**. When we begin to think we know what should have been done, and that we could have done better, we get the church and ourselves in trouble. We have too many people today who believe that the Bible is wrong and needs to be fixed. The only thing that's wrong today is people want to fix what isn't broke. The simple answer is these **people don't want to live by God's Word**; they want to do their own thing and not be condemned by the words of truth, as God had them written by Holy Ghost-anointed men of God.

Remember, God's Word is forever established in heaven, and it cannot be changed, no matter how hard men may try.

John, in this first verse, is talking about loving Jesus Christ, the only begotten Son of God. If we love Jesus, then we also love His Father, God, and if we love God, then we must also love His Son, Jesus. Many times it sounds like John is talking double talk, but we must remember that **people expressed themselves differently two thousand years ago**. I was born in 1948, we lived in the country, and since I grew up there, I can tell you we talked differently from people who lived in town. For example: I was in Lowe's buying some stuff. I gave the lady my money, and she gave me back my change. I told her, thank you muchly. She laughed and said she'd never heard anyone say that before.

Even today, people from different parts of the country talk differently and have different slang. People from the Northeast sure talk differently from the people of the South. Nevertheless, the principal thing is this, if we love God, then we will keep His commandments. By this, all men know that we love God. **It's a shame that some people who claim to be Christians don't want to live according to God's Word.** I'm brought to mind of the sixties and seventies when the charismatic movement was the big thing in the Pentecostal movements; it's a false, ungodly doctrine that did more to destroy the Pentecostal churches than anything I've known.

They preached a watered-down gospel with few if any Christian standards or convictions. There are a few good churches that call themselves charismatic, but for every good one, there's fifty that preach and believe things that aren't true.

Let me quote from the *John Phillips Commentary*: "One of the tests of maturing love is our personal attitude toward the

Bible, because in the Bible we find God's will for our lives revealed. An unsaved man considers the Bible an impossible book, mainly because he does not understand its spiritual message (1 Cor. 2:14). An immature Christian considers the demands of the Bible to be burdensome. He is somewhat like a little child who is learning to obey, and who asks, Why do I have to do that? Or wouldn't it be better to do this?

"But a Christian who experiences God's perfecting love finds himself enjoying the Word of God and truly loving it. He does not read the Bible as a textbook, but as a love letter.

"The longest chapter in the Bible is Psalms 119, and its theme is the Word of God. Every verse but two (Ps. 119:122, 132) mentions the Word of God in one form or another, as "law," "precepts," "commandments," and so forth. But the interesting thing is that the psalmist loves the Word of God and enjoys telling us about it! O how love I thy law! (Psalms 119:97)."

If we don't serve the Lord with joy, praise and worship, then we will, before long, turn our backs on God. If serving the Lord becomes grievous and burdensome, then for some reason we've let the devil steal away our confidence in God. **Without faith, hope and confidence in God, it becomes impossible to serve and please the Lord.** We serve the Lord because of the joy that comes with salvation. Do burdens and trials come our way? Yes, of course. Anyone who preaches otherwise is a liar. We are, according to the Word, going to suffer trials and temptations, but with every trial and temptation, the **Lord will make a way of escape**. However, we have to look to the Lord for that way of escape. This is one way that we have the victory over sin. God tells us in the Word that as long as we serve Him, He will be our protector.

1 Corinthians 10:13

There hath no temptation taken you but such as is common to man: but God is faithful, who will not suffer you to be tempted above that ye are able; but will with the temptation also make a way to escape, that ye may be able to bear it.

1 John 5:4-5

[4] For whatsoever is born of God overcometh the world: and this is the victory that overcometh the world, even our faith.
[5] Who is he that overcometh the world, but he that believeth that Jesus is the Son of God?

John now speaks of being an overcomer. He's not talking about a special group of people, but he's speaking of every born-again believer in Jesus Christ. We need to have identification with Jesus. **If we claim to be Christians, then we need to act like Christ acted, do as Christ did, and love as Christ loved.** Our goal is to reach the lost for Jesus. A quote from *The Wiersbe Bible Commentary* states:

"We are told that a soldier in the army of Alexander the Great was not acting bravely in battle. When he should have been pressing ahead, he was lingering behind.

"The great general approached him, and asked, 'What is your name, soldier?'

"The man replied, 'My name, sir, is Alexander.'

"The general looked him straight in the eye and said firmly, 'Soldier, get in there and fight – or change your name!'

"What's our name? 'Children of God – the born-again ones of God.' Alexander the Great wanted his name to be a symbol of courage; our name carries with it assurance of victory. To be born of God means to share God's victory.

"This is a victory of faith, but faith in what? Faith in Jesus Christ, the Son of God. The person who overcomes the world is the one 'who believes that Jesus is the Son of God.' (John 5:5 NASB). It is not faith in ourselves, but faith in Christ, that gives us the victory. 'In the world ye shall have tribulations, but be of good cheer, I have overcome the world' (John 16:33)."

The victory has already been won; it was won at Calvary. There are still some battles to be fought in our personal lives, but the outcome has already been declared. Jesus is victor; He is Lord and Master of every situation. Praise God for the victory. The world doesn't know Jesus for this reason: The sinner feels at ease in the world. The Christian, the born-again believer knows that this world isn't our home; **we're just wayfarers looking for that city whose builder and maker is God**. We're not of this world, and God calls upon us to overcome the world with all of its allures and temptations. We're to abstain from the world regardless of whether it shows us a friendly face or a face of contempt.

We, as God's children, are to know the world for what it is, the enemy of God. To get a good idea of how we should view the world, read Hebrews the eleventh chapter, the chapter on faith. We must keep the faith. **We must believe that Jesus is the only begotten Son of God, and that He is a rewarder of those who diligently seek Him and His perfect will.** *Wiersbe* says there are four stages of backsliding.

1. "Friendship with the world (James 4:4)"

2. "Spotted by the world (James 1:27)"
3. "Loving the world (1 John 2:15-17)"
4. "Conformed to the world (Romans 12:2)"

A person backslides by **not praying daily and by not reading the Word daily**. This causes them to grow cold in their souls, and then they begin to play with the world and finally give over completely and walk away from God. The last step is to recognize what has happened and not do anything about it.

Barnes' Notes states: "It is true that a man may gain a victory over one worldly passion; he may abandon the gay circle, may break away from habits of profaneness, may leave the company of the unprincipled and polluted; but still, unless he has faith in the Son of God, the spirit of the world will reign supreme in his soul in some form. The appeal which John so confidently made in his time may be as confidently made now. We may ask, as he did, where is there one who shows that he has obtained a complete victory over the world, except the true Christian."

The only way to escape this world of sin and evil is through the blood of Jesus Christ; there is no other way. The song says: "What can wash away my sins? Nothing but the blood of Jesus. What can make me whole again? Nothing but the blood of Jesus."

1 John 5:6-10

⁶ This is he that came by water and blood, even Jesus Christ; not by water only, but by water and blood. And it is the Spirit that beareth witness, because the Spirit is truth.
⁷ For there are three that bear record in heaven, the Fa-

ther, the Word, and the Holy Ghost: and these three are one.

⁸ And there are three that bear witness in earth, the Spirit, and the water, and the blood: and these three agree in one.

⁹ If we receive the witness of men, the witness of God is greater: for this is the witness of God which he hath testified of his Son.

¹⁰ He that believeth on the Son of God hath the witness in himself: he that believeth not God hath made him a liar; because he believeth not the record that God gave of his Son.

What bears witness of God's Son in this world? **It's the Holy Ghost that bears witness in the world today.** To the child of God, the Holy Ghost comes as the promised comforter. As we are filled with the Holy Ghost, the Holy Ghost will lead us into all truths; he becomes a close-knit part of our lives, and he warns us of the devil's snares. In this way, they can be avoided. The scripture speaks of the water and the blood. The water can be said to be when Jesus came to John to be baptized. John's baptism was to repentance, and **we know that Jesus had nothing to repent of**. When John fully realized who Jesus was, John told Jesus that he needed to be baptized of Jesus. But Jesus said to John, Suffer it to be so now.

Matthew 3:13-17

¹³ Then cometh Jesus from Galilee to Jordan unto John, to be baptized of him.

¹⁴ But John forbad him, saying, I have need to be baptized of thee, and comest thou to me?

15 And Jesus answering said unto him, Suffer it to be so now: for thus it becometh us to fulfil all righteousness. Then he suffered him.

16 And Jesus, when he was baptized, went up straightway out of the water: and, lo, the heavens were opened unto him, and he saw the Spirit of God descending like a dove, and lighting upon him:

17 And lo a voice from heaven, saying, This is my beloved Son, in whom I am well pleased.

There's a false teaching that says Jesus was a man like any other man. The change came when John the Baptist baptized Jesus in the Jordan River. It teaches that at the time Jesus was baptized, "the Christ" came upon Him. This spirit of Christ stayed upon Jesus until He went to the cross, where it left Him. They say that's why Jesus spoke those words, "*My God, my God, why hast thou forsaken me?*" (Matthew 27:46). Then Jesus died like any other mortal human being. There are so many false doctrines in the world today. **If we don't know the Word of God, if we don't read and study the Bible, then we fall prey to any and everything that claims to be of God.**

A little knowledge can be very dangerous to the child of God. **A little truth mixed with lies leads many, many people astray from God.** So, read and study lest you be taken by surprise to find out you've been lied to and led down the wrong path, away from the full truth of God and His plan for your life. I sometimes think of all the people who get into false beliefs and wonder how much good they could have done; how many souls they could have reached, if they hadn't followed the wrong voices. Our lives are short; **what we do for Jesus, we must do quickly**; time is running out, because Jesus is coming back for His bride.

As we study these scriptures, John is showing us that everything that happened was not by chance but by holy design. **God has a master plan for this world and the souls that are in it.** We are saved because God's spirit began to deal with us. We were called by God or drawn by God's spirit.

John 6:44

> *No man can come to me, except the Father which hath sent me draw him: and I will raise him up at the last day.*

When we feel the drawing of God's spirit, then is the time to answer the call. Many accept God's call and give their lives over to Him; but many won't say now; **rather, they want to make their decision *at some later time*, which may or may not come.** Just as in the days of Noah, God's spirit will not always strive with man, and man can and does sin away his days of grace. This isn't a popular message; people don't want to hear that they can and sometimes do reject God enough times that God will no longer deal with them, thus closing the door of salvation to them.

Genesis 6:3

> *And the LORD said, My spirit shall not always strive with man, for that he also is flesh: yet his days shall be an hundred and twenty years.*

This verse in Genesis lets us know that God can and will withdraw His spirit from us. Here in the third chapter of Genesis,

God waited one hundred and twenty years. Why? Because it took that long for Noah to build the Ark and get everything ready before the rain began to fall. Don't be blinded by what unscrupulous preachers and teachers may say. **Balance everything with the Word of God**; if a person is truly telling you the truth, they won't mind you comparing what they say with the Word of God. In fact, they should be glad and happy that you want the truth, for the truth will set you free.

John 8:32

> *And ye shall know the truth, and the truth shall make you free.*

We hear so much that God is love, and He is; that God is light, and so He is; but one thing that's important to remember is that **God is truth, and He cannot and will not condone a lie**. We can lie to those around us, we can even lie to ourselves, but there's no conceivable way that we can lie to God; it cannot be done. God let His Son die for us that we might live, but not on our terms. Only on His. Oh, the precious blood of Jesus that saves from sin, which gives eternal life.

Blood is precious when a child is conceived. Its body makes its own blood. The child doesn't use one drop of its mother's blood. They may not even be the same blood type. As adults, we can give blood to help save lives. As a regular blood donor, so far, I've personally given over ten gallons to help save many lives.

Think how special Jesus' blood was. He was conceived of the Holy Ghost, He had no earthly father and He didn't use even one drop of May's blood. He was and is the most special person who has ever lived, totally God in human form. **His blood was so special and divine that it paid the ransom for our salvation.**

In the seventh and eighth verses of the fifth chapter of 1st John, we read that there are three that bear record in heaven and three that bear witness in earth.

In Verse 7 there are three that bear record in Heaven:

1. The Father, God Himself, the creator of the world, the universe and all that therein is.

2. The Word, Jesus Christ, God's only begotten Son. He was there in the beginning when the world was formed, and He was there when God made Adam, breathed in him the breath of life and man became a living soul.

Genesis 1:26-27

26 And God said, Let us make man in our image, after our likeness: and let them have dominion over the fish of the sea, and over the fowl of the air, and over the cattle, and over all the earth, and over every creeping thing that creepeth upon the earth.
27 So God created man in his own image, in the image of God created he him; male and female created he them.

Genesis 2:7

And the LORD God formed man of the dust of the ground, and breathed into his nostrils the breath of life; and man became a living soul.

John 1:1-5

¹ In the beginning was the Word, and the Word was with God, and the Word was God.
² The same was in the beginning with God.
³ All things were made by him; and without him was not any thing made that was made.
⁴ In him was life; and the life was the light of men.
⁵ And the light shineth in darkness; and the darkness comprehended it not.

3. The Holy Ghost is the third member of the triune Godhead. Jesus said to the disciples that after He was gone back to heaven, He would pray to the Father who would send the saints another comforter, the Holy Ghost. When we are saved, our sins are forgiven, and we receive the spirit of Christ who comes into our hearts to live in us. **The Holy Ghost is separate from salvation.** We can believe in God, be saved and still not have the Holy Ghost.

Acts 19:1-7

¹ And it came to pass, that, while Apollos was at Corinth, Paul having passed through the upper coasts came to Ephesus: and finding certain disciples,
² He said unto them, Have ye received the Holy Ghost since ye believed? And they said unto him, We have not so much as heard whether there be any Holy Ghost.
³ And he said unto them, Unto what then were ye baptized? And they said, Unto John's baptism.
⁴ Then said Paul, John verily baptized with the baptism of

repentance, saying unto the people, that they should be-lieve on him which should come after him, that is, on Christ Jesus.

⁵ When they heard this, they were baptized in the name of the Lord Jesus.

⁶ And when Paul had laid his hands upon them, the Holy Ghost came on them; and they spake with tongues, and prophesied.

⁷ And all the men were about twelve.

The Holy Ghost is the third person of the trinity. He works with God the Father and Jesus Christ, but the Holy Ghost isn't the spirit of God, nor is He the spirit of Christ. He is His own person, separate from God and Jesus. When people study the scriptures, they see that **the spirit of God and the Holy Ghost are not the same**. Those who say that the spirit of God is the same do a dishonor to the Holy Ghost.

John 14:26

But the Comforter, which is the Holy Ghost, whom the Father will send in my name, he shall teach you all things, and bring all things to your remembrance, whatsoever I have said unto you.

John 15:26

But when the Comforter is come, whom I will send unto you from the Father, even the Spirit of truth, which proceedeth from the Father, he shall testify of me:

2 Corinthians 13:14

The grace of the Lord Jesus Christ, and the love of God, and the communion of the Holy Ghost, be with you all. Amen.

There are three separate individuals with one purpose, one goal in mind, working together and making up the Godhead. Three in one and one in three, **separate yet not separate individuals**. These are *"they which bear record in heaven."*

Where Verse 7 tells us that as there are three that bear record in heaven. In Verse 8, the three that bear witness in the earth agree in one.

Verse 8 states that there are three that bear witness in the earth.

1. The spirit of God is at work in this world, to lead men and women to Jesus Christ. No one can come to Jesus and accept Him as their Savior, except the spirit of God does a work in their hearts and draw them to repentance. We hear people say, "Well, I had gone as far as I could go, so I decided to give God a try." That sounds good, but we don't decide when we'll get saved. It's not up to us. God's spirit must be drawing us to God, or there's no salvation. Salvation isn't a whim; it's very serious. Don't take God lightly; your soul is at risk. Too many are playing church. Too many ministers are making it their life's goal to make people feel good about themselves and not preaching or teaching the truth. What good does it do to make people feel good about themselves and do nothing about their soul's condition? We miss the mark when we do nothing for the soul. I can tell you how good you are, I can pat you on the back and sing your praises, but all of it means nothing until you meet Jesus and make Him the Lord of your life. That only happens when the spirit draws you to meet with God.

2. The water is the second witness. It refers to water baptism. John the Baptist baptized for the remission of sin. Jesus came to the river to be baptized by John. Why was this done? It was to set an example for the children of God to follow. At the river when Jesus was baptized, God spoke out of heaven, "*This is my beloved Son in whom I am well pleased*," and then the Holy Ghost descended out of heaven in the form of a dove. Thus, all three were there at the Jordan River, Jesus, God and the Holy Ghost, when Jesus was baptized. Is water baptism necessary for a man to go to heaven? No, it is not. It's a symbol to those around us that we are saved and on our way to heaven. Water baptism does not and cannot save us. After we are saved and born again, then and only then should we be baptized. As we are baptized, going down into the water symbolizes the death and burial of Jesus Christ; when we are raised out of the water, it symbolizes the new birth in Jesus Christ. The baptizer, the one who lifts you out of the water, is the symbol of God's hand raising Jesus from the dead. Why should we be baptized? Baptism is the outward show to those who are around us that we have found Jesus real in our lives, that we've become believers in Christ and our sins washed away or covered in Christ's blood. Water baptism is a symbol of our faith. There's no saving power in water; there's no life in the water; there is life in the blood. The blood changes us, as we believe. Remember when Philip met the Ethiopian eunuch and he preached to him Jesus? As they went, they came to water, and the

195

eunuch wanted to be baptized. What did Philip say? He told him, *"If thou believest with all thine heart, thou mayest."*

Acts 8:34-37

34 And the eunuch answered Philip, and said, I pray thee, of whom speaketh the prophet this? of himself, or of some other man?
35 Then Philip opened his mouth, and began at the same scripture, and preached unto him Jesus.
36 And as they went on their way, they came unto a certain water: and the eunuch said, See, here is water; what doth hinder me to be baptized?
37 And Philip said, If thou believest with all thine heart, thou mayest. And he answered and said, I believe that Jesus Christ is the Son of God.

We read in Mark 16:16, where Jesus is speaking: *"He that believeth and is baptized shall be saved; but he that believeth not shall be damned."* **The first thing a person must do is believe Jesus is the Son of God and accept Him as their Savior.** Then they can be baptized, but as scripture states, *"but he that believeth not shall be damned."* Too many times people have gone into the water a dry sinner and have come up a wet sinner, for they never truly believed.

3. The blood is the third witness. The blood of Jesus Christ was shed for the forgiveness of sin. For without the shedding of the blood, there can be no forgiveness. From the beginning, there was the shedding of the blood. God made clothes for Adam and Eve out of animal skins – the shedding of blood;

Abel's sacrifice – again, the shedding of blood; God supplying the lamb for Abraham – the shedding of blood. The priestly duties – the shedding of blood. All the way to the days of Jesus, there was the shedding of the blood. Until finally, we reached the last and most special sacrifice, the shedding of the blood of Jesus, the Christ, for the remission of the sins of the world.

All three of these bear witness in earth, and these three agree in one. What do they agree to? It's very simple. They agree to the fact that **Jesus is the truth, the life and the way** and that no man goes to heaven except through Jesus Christ, God's only begotten Son. **Jesus' blood tore down all the barriers that stood between God and us.** Now we don't need a priest to go to God for us; we can go directly to the throne of grace, because Jesus paid the ransom for our souls.

One more thing that the shedding of Jesus's blood did was to open the door to the Gentile world. It brought access to God out into the open and to the world. Before the death of Jesus, God was closed off to the world, separated behind a vail, while Jesus' death, in the open and before the world, paid the awful price. **The death of Jesus on the cross opened up salvation to every man, woman and child** in the entire world. These three agree that Jesus is the Son of God, and there is no other.

In Verse 9 we read about the witness of men. If we stop and think, nearly everything we know today is by the witness of men. We have either heard it or read it at some time. All this information is stored away in our brains. A good ninety percent is useless to us in our everyday lives. Our heads are full of information on sports, history, politics and such that we will never use. Another good example is the theory of evolution; man is trying to force everyone to believe in evolution. However, **evolution is**

simply a theory without any facts to back it up. We are being bombarded every day to believe in something that cannot be proven. Fact or fiction, the witness of men pushes us to believe in falsehoods, in man's wisdom; but **no matter how smart man gets, there are still age-old questions man cannot answer**.

To quote *John Phillips*:

"It is against this background of our receiving the witness of humans that John introduces his telling argument: 'The witness of God is greater.' The Word of God must take precedence over the word of people – because people make mistakes; they are finite and are often wrong. God is omniscient and makes no mistakes. He speaks with authority. The Bible is true – and it is absolutely incumbent upon us that we believe the Lord Jesus Christ and accept God's Word at its face value.

"In other words, we must believe God's witness and especially His witness concerning His Son. God's Word is the absolute, inerrant, and infallible truth, and when its teachings conflict with teachings of men, we must believe God.

"The greatest insult we can offer to anyone is to say, 'I don't believe you,' or 'I cannot trust you.' Yet millions daily offer that insult to God, accepting the witness of men and repudiating the witness of God. An unbeliever once said to D. L. Moody, 'But, Mr. Moody, I can't believe.' 'Young man,' said Mr. Moody, 'Whom can't you believe?' To tell God you don't believe what He says betrays a desperate state of soul.

"Thus, John lays out the credibility of the witness. We are not being asked to believe the unreasonable; we are, however, confronted with the greatest information ever presented to the human race. And it is true! This witness carried its own commendation – divine revelation is as far above human reasoning as the heavens are high above the earth."

The witness of God is the greatest witness that a person can have. **The devil tries to bring in doubt**; he tries to get us to deny what God has done. There have been several times of trial and persecution where the devil almost made me doubt whether I was saved. However, always remember this: *"greater is He that is in you, than he that is in the world."* And that with every temptation that comes our way, God will also send to us a way of escape (1 Corinthians 10:13 . . . *who will not suffer you to be tempted above that ye are able; but will with the temptation also make a way to escape, that ye may be able to bear it*), so that we be not overwhelmed by Satan. **The witness of God is far greater than the witness of men.** Believe God, hold to your faith, stand in the face of the world and God will give to you the victory.

Believe God, let God be truth, and every man be a liar. The assurance of salvation is ours; it belongs to us, but **we must reach out, grasp it and hold to it lest the enemy take it from us**. Many a battle has been lost because we haven't taken the opportunities that God has given. Walmart has a saying they teach their employees: "We don't have problems; we have opportunities." We need to apply this in our lives. Our attitude needs to be, "We don't have any defeats; we only have victories in Jesus Christ our Lord." **If a person believes they will be defeated by the devil, then they will be, because they'll give up without a fight.** If we believe we are victorious through Christ Jesus, then we will be victorious, for Jesus fights our battles with us.

1 John 5:11-13

[11] And this is the record, that God hath given to us eternal

life, and this life is in his Son.
[12] He that hath the Son hath life; and he that hath not the
Son of God hath not life.
[13] These things have I written unto you that believe on the
name of the Son of God; that ye may know that ye have
eternal life, and that ye may believe on the name of the
Son of God.

The one thing that we must hold onto is the record that God has given to the children of God. From the time of Adam, God has been keeping a book of record. In this record, it tells us of the history of man, his victories and his defeats:

1. The fall of Cain
2. The friendship of Enoch, how he walked with God and how Enoch was a perfect man in God's sight
3. The destruction of the world by water, where only eight souls escaped; and Noah being a just man, perfect in his generation, who walked with God (Genesis 6:9)
4. The story of Exodus from Egyptian bondage
5. The story of Joshua in the promised land
6. How the prophets obeyed God
7. How God blessed obedience
8. How God punished disobedience
9. All the way up to Jesus being born the Savior of the world
10. The life and ministry of Jesus
11. His death on the cross
12. The resurrection from the dead

13. Jesus leaving to go back into heaven

14. The ministry of the Apostles

All of this is the record that God has given. This record was given to encourage us, to bless us, and to give us hope and faith in God and His dear Son, Jesus. We could go on and on about the record that God gives us of the preaching of the Apostles and the miracles that God performed as the Apostles believed in God and His power; and how Paul, before he was beheaded, said that he was ready and gave his testimony to encourage us and strengthen us in this battle that we fight for the Lord.

2 Timothy 4:6-8

> *6 For I am now ready to be offered, and the time of my departure is at hand.*
> *7 I have fought a good fight, I have finished my course, I have kept the faith:*
> *8 Henceforth there is laid up for me a crown of righteousness, which the Lord, the righteous judge, shall give me at that day: and not to me only, but unto all them also that love his appearing.*

In this struggle, at stake are our souls and where we will spend eternity; the gift of eternal life with Christ is our reward; don't throw it away.

Think of all the titles that have been given to Jesus. He's been called the King of the Jews, the Son of Man, the Son of God, and he is called our Righteousness. He is our Mediator, the Creator, the Lamb of God, the King of kings, the Lord of lords, the

Lilly of the Valley, and the Bright and Morning Star. The list goes on and on. If we seek to spend eternity with Jesus, **we must believe that He's the only true Son of God**. Let all men be liars, but let God's Word forever remain true.

There's a longing inside each human being whether they'll admit it or not. That longing is to live forever in a state of bliss and happiness. **The Christian religion is the only religion that has a Savior that's alive and not dead.** Some people have hundreds of gods; we have only one God, the true God. We worship God and His Son who gave His life so that we may spend eternity in the blessedness of heaven. The world hates and fears death, because to them, death is the end; there is no more life. However, to the child of God, we have no morbid fear of death. Scripture states that to live is Christ but to die is gain.

Philippians 1:20-21

> [20] *According to my earnest expectation and my hope, that in nothing I shall be ashamed, but that with all boldness, as always, so now also Christ shall be magnified in my body, whether it be by life, or by death.*
> [21] *For to me to live is Christ, and to die is gain.*

Can we say we're not afraid to die? Everyone dreads the unknown, simply because we've never been there before. However, to the child of God, we don't fear death, because we know what's going to happen. We will exhale on this side and inhale on the other side in the presence of Jesus our Lord. The only change to this is if Jesus comes after His bride; **then we will be "raptured" or caught away to meet Him in the air.** John goes on to say, "*I have written all these things to you who believe that Jesus is the Christ, God's only son. I tell you that as a true believer in Jesus Christ, we have prepared for us a home in heaven, reserved for us that where Jesus is, there we may be also.*"

John 14:1-4

¹ Let not your heart be troubled: ye believe in God, believe also in me.
² In my Father's house are many mansions: if it were not so, I would have told you. I go to prepare a place for you.
³ And if I go and prepare a place for you, I will come again, and receive you unto myself; that where I am, there ye may be also.
⁴ And whither I go ye know, and the way ye know.

1 Peter 1:3-5

³ Blessed be the God and Father of our Lord Jesus Christ, which according to his abundant mercy hath begotten us again unto a lively hope by the resurrection of Jesus Christ from the dead,
⁴ To an inheritance incorruptible, and undefiled, and that fadeth not away, reserved in heaven for you,
⁵ Who are kept by the power of God through faith unto salvation ready to be revealed in the last time.

I don't know about you, but I'm looking for that great homecoming where we will meet once again with all our loved ones who have gone on before us. What a time that will be to see Jesus face to face!

1 John 5:14-15

[14] And this is the confidence that we have in him, that, if we ask any thing according to his will, he heareth us: [15] And if we know that he hear us, whatsoever we ask, we know that we have the petitions that we desired of him.

One thing that's vital in serving God is that we must learn to trust Him in every problem and in every trial. Only when we learn to trust God can we have confidence in God. Confidence in God is like faith in God. Confidence is going to God without any doubt, knowing that He hears and answers prayer. In this life, everyone needs someone to confide in, to tell their problems to. They may not be able to help, but just to have someone they can talk to; someone they can tell their secrets to, knowing they will never tell anyone. They may not be able to help, but they know how to listen; and sometimes, **all people need is a good listener**. We all need to "vent" from time to time. So, be a good listener, and show Godly love and compassion. Be a Christian friend, and in love, help when you can; **be there for those who don't know where to go**. You will find that God will open doors you may have thought would never be opened.

As we serve God and stand firm for God and His kingdom, we will gain an ever-growing confidence in Him. As we pray and believe, **we'll see God answer prayer after prayer**, and with each prayer answered, our confidence will grow. The world refuses to accept the fact that as Christians pray, God hears and answers their prayers. I hear people in the world say that God has never answered their prayers. Then when I ask them if they go to church and live a consistent Christian life, they offer up an excuse for why they don't go to church and why they don't live a Christian life.

We must stress that **to have God answer our prayers, we must serve Him**; if we don't live our lives for God, there's no reason why God should answer our prayers. To the Christian, God has promised to meet our needs, not give us our wants. (Philippians 4:19 – *But my God shall supply all your need according to his riches in glory by Christ Jesus.*) There's a difference between needs and wants; **just because you want something doesn't mean you need it**. There are two reasons why we don't get our prayers answered: because we ask not, and because we ask amiss.

James 4:3

> *Ye ask, and receive not, because ye ask amiss, that ye may consume it upon your lusts.*

What is "asking amiss"? It's when we seek God for **things that we don't need or that may be harmful to us in our future**. You see, God loves us the way a mother and dad love their children. He only wants the very best for us, because we are His children. When we pray, ask in faith believing that we shall have what we've prayed for.

If we look at God's Word, we find all the way through where and how God answered prayer. It may also surprise some people to look through the pages of history where God answered prayer after prayer for his people. **Prayer is the one thing that keeps us walking in the love and power of God.** So, pray, pray, pray, "Oh, God have your will."

1 John 5:16-19

^{16} If any man see his brother sin a sin which is not unto death, he shall ask, and he shall give him life for them that sin not unto death. There is a sin unto death: I do not say that he shall pray for it.
^{17} All unrighteousness is sin: and there is a sin not unto death.
^{18} We know that whosoever is born of God sinneth not; but he that is begotten of God keepeth himself, and that wicked one toucheth him not.
^{19} And we know that we are of God, and the whole world lieth in wickedness.

A Christian faces many enemies on earth. Every day we're confronted on every hand by the wickedness of this world. We're confronted on the job, in the stores, by advertising from newspapers to television; in fact, just about everywhere we look, we see the allure of this wicked world. This allure of people having so much fun, enjoying themselves – and I will agree that there's a momentary pleasure in the world – however, how do they feel when the fun is over and reality sets back in? I can tell you, because I've been there. **When the fun's over, they're right back where they started from.**

The same old problems are staring them right in the face, and they think, "Now what am I going to do?" They start looking for something to do that will make them forget again for a short while. It's the same old rat race over again. There's no peace, no contentment; their mind is in turmoil. The devil tells them to try this or try that, and so they do. Everything is a short-term fix, but they cannot find that perfect peace. The world has nothing to offer that's permanent. The only permanent peace comes from God, through His Son, Jesus. **With Jesus, there's peace in our heart no matter the storms of life.** How, you ask, can this peace stay, and the answer is simple. Because the world didn't give it to us, and the world sure can't take it away. The only way to lose the peace of God is to turn our back on Him and walk away. Believe it or not, some people do. They go right back into what God brought them out of.

What can we do? The Word tells us that if we see our brothers and sisters sin, we are to pray for them; to go before God and ask Him to deal with their hearts; to bring them to repentance. We are to open their eyes to what they're doing before they've gone too far to return. You see, Cain was wrong; **we are our brother's keeper in the spirit**. We cannot make people live right, but we can talk to them about their soul's condition; and after that we can pray, pray, and pray some more.

Prayer works, and prayer changes things. Sin is the downfall of every man, woman and child; the nature of man is to do evil things, things that are not Godly. Despite the many good people we might know, no matter how morally good a person is, if they haven't given their heart and life to Jesus, they are a sinner, and no sinner goes to heaven. It may not seem right, but without a born-again experience, no one can go to heaven. Sin is sin, and sin stands between us and God. No matter how much God loves us, and He does far more than we can imagine, when God looks at us, He sees the sin, and no sin can be allowed to enter heaven. However, there's good news! **God will forgive sin if we truly repent and ask Him to.** All sin can be forgiven, except one; there is a sin unto death, a sin that God will not and cannot forgive. That sin is the sin against the Holy Ghost.

Matthew 12:31-32

31 Wherefore I say unto you, All manner of sin and blasphemy shall be forgiven unto men: but the blasphemy against the Holy Ghost shall not be forgiven unto men.
32 And whosoever speaketh a word against the Son of man, it shall be forgiven him: but whosoever speaketh against the Holy Ghost, it shall not be forgiven him, neither in this world, neither in the world to come.

There are many different opinions as to what this blasphemy against the Holy Ghost truly is. **It partly depends on what denomination you belong to as to what you are taught to believe.** In my book, *A Study on the Holy Ghost*, it states the following:

"Blasphemy against the Holy Ghost, in my opinion and according to scripture, is this: After a person has been enlightened, has tasted of the heavenly gift, and has been made a partaker of the Holy Ghost, if they deny the reality of their experiences, they have committed blasphemy. These are the people who know what it is to be saved and set free from sin, to be filled with the Holy Ghost and feel the very presence of God. If, knowing all that has happened to them, they turn their backs on God and publicly deny all they have experienced, saying, 'God is not real; the Holy Ghost baptism isn't real. It's all lies,' is blasphemy against the Holy Ghost and will never be forgiven in this world, neither will it be forgiven in the world to come."

The Holy Ghost is the most sensitive member of the Godhead, and to sin against Him is the sin unto death.

The children of God are saved to serve God and let their

light shine into the darkness of sin. We are to abstain from the very appearance of evil; we are not to do the things that the world does. Sin condemns the soul of man; the grace of God sets man free from the death of sin. **Sin is the thing that will keep a person from going to heaven.** The scripture warns us what to stay away from.

Romans 1:21-32

21 Because that, when they knew God, they glorified him not as God, neither were thankful; but became vain in their imaginations, and their foolish heart was darkened.

22 Professing themselves to be wise, they became fools,

23 And changed the glory of the uncorruptible God into an image made like to corruptible man, and to birds, and fourfooted beasts, and creeping things.

24 Wherefore God also gave them up to uncleanness through the lusts of their own hearts, to dishonour their own bodies between themselves:

25 Who changed the truth of God into a lie, and worshipped and served the creature more than the Creator, who is blessed for ever. Amen.

26 For this cause God gave them up unto vile affections: for even their women did change the natural use into that which is against nature:

27 And likewise also the men, leaving the natural use of the woman, burned in their lust one toward another; men with men working that which is unseemly, and receiving in themselves that recompence of their error which was meet.

28 And even as they did not like to retain God in their

knowledge, God gave them over to a reprobate mind, to do those things which are not convenient;

29 Being filled with all unrighteousness, fornication, wickedness, covetousness, maliciousness; full of envy, murder, debate, deceit, malignity; whisperers,

30 Backbiters, haters of God, despiteful, proud, boasters, inventors of evil things, disobedient to parents,

31 Without understanding, covenantbreakers, without natural affection, implacable, unmerciful:

32 Who knowing the judgment of God, that they which commit such things are worthy of death, not only do the same, but have pleasure in them that do them.

1 Corinthians 6:9-10

9 Know ye not that the unrighteous shall not inherit the kingdom of God? Be not deceived: neither fornicators, nor idolaters, nor adulterers, nor effeminate, nor abusers of themselves with mankind,

10 Nor thieves, nor covetous, nor drunkards, nor revilers, nor extortioners, shall inherit the kingdom of God.

Galatians 5:19-21

19 Now the works of the flesh are manifest, which are these; Adultery, fornication, uncleanness, lasciviousness,

20 Idolatry, witchcraft, hatred, variance, emulations, wrath, strife, seditions, heresies,

21 Envyings, murders, drunkenness, revellings, and such like: of the which I tell you before, as I have also told you in time past, that they which do such things shall not in-

herit the kingdom of God.

Colossians 3:5-9

⁵ Mortify therefore your members which are upon the earth; fornication, uncleanness, inordinate affection, evil concupiscence, and covetousness, which is idolatry:
⁶ For which things' sake the wrath of God cometh on the children of disobedience:
⁷ In the which ye also walked some time, when ye lived in them.
⁸ But now ye also put off all these; anger, wrath, malice, blasphemy, filthy communication out of your mouth.
⁹ Lie not one to another, seeing that ye have put off the old man with his deeds;

Revelation 21:8

But the fearful, and unbelieving, and the abominable, and murderers, and whoremongers, and sorcerers, and idolaters, and all liars, shall have their part in the lake which burneth with fire and brimstone: which is the second death.

1 John 5:20-21

²⁰ And we know that the Son of God is come, and hath given us an understanding, that we may know him that is true, and we are in him that is true, even in his Son Jesus Christ. This is the true God, and eternal life.
²¹ Little children, keep yourselves from idols. Amen.

Jesus has come to the earth to set men free from bondage. He offers a freedom like no other can, a chance to know God on a one-on-one basis. With God, there are no priests, no hierarchies; we can talk straight to God, and no one has to talk for us. Those who serve idols become like the gods they serve. They become indifferent to the feelings of those around them. When we look at the gods of the past and present, most are made of wood, stone, silver, brass and gold; but these gods are powerless; they cannot see, hear or move, because they are made by man, and they have no life.

These idols are the product of someone's imagination or statues of some man or beast; but **these gods are all dead**. They cannot save, heal or work miracles. They have no power. The Christian religion is the only group of worshippers whose God is alive, who hears our prayers, who sees our problems and helps make a way for His children. **Our God can and does heal and work miracles on our behalf.** Christians who have met the one, the only true God, know what it's like to be loved by God. We have a loving and compassionate Savior.

We serve Him out of a heart of love, a love born not of this world, but a love that comes from heaven above. When everything else is laid aside, here's the truth of it all. There's only one God; there's only one Savior and one Holy Ghost. All else is falsehood. **There's only one way to go to heaven, and that's through the shed blood of Jesus Christ**; there is no other way. Man is only trying to fool himself when he claims otherwise. It certainly doesn't help when backslidden preachers preach and teach a form of godliness, but they deny the power thereof. There's life in Jesus Christ, God's only Son. All else is lies, blasphemy and a reproach. Serve God, trust in Jesus and live.

Chapter 5 – Test Your Knowledge

1. Many Bible scholars believe that the first three verses of Chapter 5 really should be

_____

2. What is the principal thing that we will keep if we love God? _____

3. What are the three things we must have to serve the Lord?

_____

_____

_____

4. Christians must have identification with

_____

5. If we claim to be Christians, what are the three things we are to do?

_____

_____

_____

6. It is not faith in ourselves, but faith in Christ that

_____

7. To the child of God, the Holy Ghost comes as a

_____

8. A little knowledge is a very

_____

9. What, if anything, can a man or woman sin away?

_____

_____

10. In Genesis, Chapter Six, why did God wait one hundred twenty years?

_____

_____

_____

11. When a child is conceived, how much of its mother's blood is used to form that child?

_____

_____

12. What three bear record in heaven?

_____

_____

_____

13. What three bear witness in earth?

_____

_____

_____

14. Is evolution a fact or a theory?

_____

15. If a person believes they will be defeated by the devil, then they _____

_____

16. A Christian must have _____ in God.

17. What are the two reasons prayers are not answered?

_____

_____

18. Where is the only place to find permanent peace?

_____

_____

18. What sin can never be forgiven?

_____

_____

19. There is only one way to go to heaven. What must we go through to get there?

_____

_____

_____

_____

_____

2nd John

Introduction to 2nd John

For this second letter, John addresses himself as "the elder." Much has been said about John not giving his name, and some use this to claim that John didn't write this epistle. Nevertheless, most Bible scholars agree that John wrote this epistle. Even though John only called himself the elder, everyone knew who the elder was; it was the great apostle John. John was the last one of the twelve disciples called by Jesus to be alive; history has it that John lived to be of a great age. John was the last one who walked and talked with Jesus. Therefore, you could say that John knew Jesus as much as any of the other disciples. John was a fisherman who became a disciple of John the Baptist and followed him until Jesus came to be baptized by John. Afterward, John left the Baptist and began following Jesus.

John was an eyewitness to all that Jesus said and did. He was there when the water was turned into wine at the marriage in Cana of Galilee. He was there when Jesus healed the sick and when demons were cast out of the possessed. John saw the dead raised and brought back to life, and he watched as Jesus took a boy's meal and blessed it so that the multitude of people were fed. He watched as Jesus came to the disciples walking upon the water. John was a witness to the three-and-one-half years of Jesus' ministry. John was with the other disciples when Jesus appeared to them after He was raised from the dead; he was there as Jesus was taken into heaven. John was among the hundred and twenty to receive the Holy Ghost on the Day of Pentecost.

Later John was moved upon by the Holy Ghost to write the Book of Saint John. Later still, Jesus appeared to John when John was in the spirit and had John write the Revelation that God had given to Jesus. Even later in life, John was moved upon to write the Epistles of First, Second and Third John. I'm sure that John wrote many letters to different ones; however, God didn't see fit to have them become part of the Holy Bible. To think of all the things that John saw and heard Jesus say and do is enough to boggle the mind. Of the twelve disciples, Jesus had an inner circle made up of Peter, James and John. These three were with Jesus on the mountain of transfiguration to witness the glory of God. Is it any wonder why John's ministry was so great?

In the second epistle that John wrote, he's writing to the "elect lady" and her children. There are differences among Bible scholars as to who this elect lady might be; some believe that John is writing to a woman he knew, while others believe John is writing to one of the local churches in the area. I am also of the opinion that this letter was written to one of the local churches and not to a certain woman and her family. John is trying to give words of encouragement to this church and its members, while at the same time giving them a warning about deceivers coming into the churches, deceivers who profess to be good Christians but in truth do not believe the true gospel. John calls these individuals antichrist because they preach and teach a perverted gospel. They have a form of godliness but deny the truth of God's Word.

Gnosticism was working its way into the churches. There were several forms of Gnosticism, and each form was a threat to the true gospel of Jesus Christ. The Christian movement was still young, and the apostles were all gone except for John. John was worried about the future of the fledgling Christian churches. He knew that Satan was working hard to deceive and destroy the messengers and the gospel. Things haven't changed; even today, Satan is trying to destroy the church of Jesus Christ. As we look around us, we can see forms of Gnosticism in the church world today, and it's just as dangerous to the church now as it was in John's day.

Acts 20:28-30

> *28 Take heed therefore unto yourselves, and to all the flock, over the which the Holy Ghost hath made you overseers, to feed the church of God, which he hath purchased with his own blood.*
> *29 For I know this, that after my departing shall grievous wolves enter in among you, not sparing the flock.*
> *30 Also of your own selves shall men arise, speaking perverse things, to draw away disciples after them.*

2nd John

2 John 1:1-3

¹ The elder unto the elect lady and her children, whom I love in the truth; and not I only, but also all they that have known the truth;
² For the truth's sake, which dwelleth in us, and shall be with us for ever.
³ Grace be with you, mercy, and peace, from God the Father, and from the Lord Jesus Christ, the Son of the Father, in truth and love.

One of the main targets of the devil is the home, especially Christian homes. **If the devil can disrupt the home, he wins.** The old saying is very true. *As the home goes, also goes the church and the nation.* The home is the key to the local church and to the nation as a whole.

In this letter, John addresses himself as the elder. **There's no doubt that John is the writer of this letter.** John addresses this writing to the elect lady and her children. It's believed that the elect lady is one of the many local churches in the area. Her children would then be the true believers who made up that local church. John tells the church that he loves his Christian brothers and sisters in Jesus Christ with a holy and God-like love, and that all brothers and sisters in the Lord should love each other with a Christian love, a Christ-like love.

The church is made up of many members, and we are the bride of Christ, so **it's very fitting that local churches would be called she, or the elect lady**. The word elect means one who has made everything right with God.

John, in these first three verses, speaks much of the truth, because God is truth, and as God is truth, we must dwell in the truth and walk in the truth. **The truth of God is what has set us free from the sin and bondage that Satan had put us in.** Where there's freedom, people think for themselves and act accordingly. However, under bondage, people are like cattle; they go where they're driven, they do as they're told, and they don't think for themselves. Those who fight the system are hated just as Christ was hated. **The truth of God's Word is under attack today just as it was when Jesus walked the shores of Galilee.** We are under attack by the world, which hates us; we are under attack by our own government, which wants to muzzle the church and to stop the truth of God's Word from being preached, so that it can carry out its agenda, its master plan to control every phase of people's lives, even what they believe in. Religion is all right as long as the government controls what's being preached from behind the pulpits of America and what's being taught in church curriculum, because they know that the truth sets men free.

The greatest truth is that Jesus Christ, God's only Son, died that mankind might be set free from sin and shame. Karl Marx wrote: "The first requisite for the people's happiness is the abolition of religion." (Quoted from *The Wiersbe Bible Commentary*.) Karl Marx knew that to fool the people into a false since of security, the first thing that had to be done was to get rid of the truth of the Gospel, because the preaching of the truth opens men's eyes to sin and the result of what sin does to the human man. The time has come that judgement must begin at the house of the Lord.

1 Peter 4:17-18

[17] *For the time is come that judgment must begin at the house of God: and if it first begin at us, what shall the end be of them that obey not the gospel of God?*
[18] *And if the righteous scarcely be saved, where shall the ungodly and the sinner appear?*

The day is far spent, the darkness approaches, let us work while there is still time and opportunity. There are souls to be reached with the Word of God.

2 John 1:4-6

[4] *I rejoiced greatly that I found of thy children walking in truth, as we have received a commandment from the Father.*
[5] *And now I beseech thee, lady, not as though I wrote a new commandment unto thee, but that which we had from the beginning, that we love one another.*
[6] *And this is love, that we walk after his commandments. This is the commandment, That, as ye have heard from the beginning, ye should walk in it.*

In the fourth verse, John bears record of the children of the elect lady. The elect lady is one of the local churches, but we don't know to which church John is referring. However, as John is writing, he's commending the believers of this church on their character and their behavior before the public. **John is greatly impressed in the manner in which they conduct themselves and the standards that they hold and live by.** John saw that they were obeying the gospel which was preached unto them. It was plain they loved the brethren, and they also showed forth a Christ-like love to and for those around them.

Nevertheless, what John most liked was their love for the truth. As we can attest, the truth will set you free. John repeatedly stresses that, as Christians, we should and must love one another, for it's impossible to keep the commandments without a true love for God and His Dear Son, Jesus Christ.

John 14:15

If ye love me, keep my commandments.

In the book of Saint John, we find these words. It's important that we note that John didn't say these words, nor did Peter, nor did Paul, nor James or any other apostle. **These words were spoken by Jesus**, Himself. That's how important John 14:15 is. There's no truthful way a man can say he loves Jesus and not keep His commandments. **If a man loves God, then of a truth, his heart's desire is to please the Lord in any way possible.** Love is long-suffering and flaunteth not itself. As scripture so plainly says, how can a man or woman not love the brotherhood and still say he or she loves God? It's totally impossible. If we love God, then we love our brothers and sisters in Christ.

1 Peter 1:7-9

⁷ That the trial of your faith, being much more precious than of gold that perisheth, though it be tried with fire, might be found unto praise and honour and glory at the appearing of Jesus Christ:

⁸ Whom having not seen, ye love; in whom, though now ye see him not, yet believing, ye rejoice with joy unspeakable and full of glory:

⁹ Receiving the end of your faith, even the salvation of your souls.

2 John 1:7-11

⁷ For many deceivers are entered into the world, who confess not that Jesus Christ is come in the flesh. This is a deceiver and an antichrist.

⁸ Look to yourselves, that we lose not those things which we have wrought, but that we receive a full reward.

⁹ Whosoever transgresseth, and abideth not in the doctrine of Christ, hath not God. He that abideth in the doctrine of Christ, he hath both the Father and the Son.

¹⁰ If there come any unto you, and bring not this doctrine, receive him not into your house, neither bid him God speed:

¹¹ For he that biddeth him God speed is partaker of his evil deeds.

John begins by giving a warning to the church. He warns that there are many, many deceivers in this ungodly world, whose aim is to destroy the church of the living God. Beware, lest you find yourself caught in the snare of the devil. Who are these deceivers? **Too many times they are people who have come out of the church, ministers and others who find it easier to play up to people and what these people want.** John says, *"They went out from us, but they were not of us."*

1 John 2:19

> *They went out from us, but they were not of us; for if they had been of us, they would no doubt have continued with us: but they went out, that they might be made manifest that they were not all of us.*

We are also to take warning of those around us and **be aware of what they say**. Another verse we need to consider is *"of your own selves shall men arise, speaking perverse things."*

Acts 20:30

> *Also of your own selves shall men arise, speaking perverse things, to draw away disciples after them.*

Take warning, **Satan is out to destroy the saints from the outside by tricking them from the inside**. Beware, lest you fall into wicked places. To quote from *John Phillips Commentary*:

"There were many such 'deceivers' abroad at the end of the apostolic era . . . . These cultists did not agree with the revealed New Testament doctrine, based upon historical fact, that the person known as Jesus Christ 'is come in the flesh,' that He was a true human being. The Docetic Gnostics thought that it was

228

outrageous to believe that the infinite God would allow Himself to be born just as all human beings are born, that He would actually become for a time, humanly speaking, a helpless infant, and that He would subject Himself to human limitations. They denied not only the fact of the Incarnation but also its possibility at any time, their denial thus including the Second Advent as well.

"Deceivers thrive, too, in the twenty-first century. The denial of the Incarnation is common today among liberal theologians. Much modern unbelief stems from the popular acceptance of the mechanistic theory of evolution, which denies the supernatural or any interference on the part of a Supreme Being on the developing order. Thus it is well to heed John's warnings."

In *Webster's Dictionary*, mechanistic is "of or in accordance with the theory of mechanism." The theory of mechanism is "the theory or doctrine that all the phenomena of the universe, particularly life, can ultimately be explained in terms of matter moving in accordance with the laws of nature."

An antichrist is someone who goes against Jesus Christ and His teachings. An example is someone who is either pro-government or anti-government. Anti- is to be of an opposite opinion. You can well believe that there are many antichristians in the world today, and even many in the church. In plain language, if you don't believe the true, unperverted gospel, you're antichrist, because you go against God's Word. I heard a preacher who said, "I don't believe everything in the Bible." That man is an antichrist. **You either believe it all, or you don't believe any of it.** In this day and hour, we see so many who are departing from the truth, being led astray by our enemy, Satan.

John again warns that the saints should be on guard, because the devil is trying to steal away the truth of God's Word from their hearts. The saints needed to obey the teachings of God's Word but at the same time remember that **the devil will sometimes appear as an angel of light**. Be careful in all things, showing forth a Christ-like spirit and giving glory to God for the good as well as the bad. Yes, we are to thank God for the bad as well as the good, because **we learn valuable lessons from the bad that comes our way**. The local churches were to show fellowship to those who came their way. Sometimes it might be a preacher who was traveling through the country, preaching God's Word; the saints welcomed visitors because they would bring news from other places about what was happening in those places.

There were times when the persons passing through were not what they professed to be. These visitors could be false teachers spreading an unholy gospel. Therefore, care was always to be taken. John stresses on no account was a visitor to be taken at face value. If these people were imposters, it would soon come into the light. **No matter how good a person may act, God will bring out the truth of their character for all to see.** Beware lest these counterfeits of Satan lead people astray with their false doctrine.

Now we come back again to the question of whether a believer can backslide and lose their salvation. Many Bible scholars say no, that once you're saved you will be forever saved. Others believe that, yes, you can lose your salvation by walking away from God and going back into the world, to a life of sin and shame. What do I believe? I believe that yes you can walk away from God and His gift of salvation. **Many scriptures teach that a man can turn away from God's grace and lose their salvation.** From the Old Testament through the New Testament, we find by searching the scripture, that the saints can and do lose their salvation.

Ezekiel 18:19-32

¹⁹ Yet say ye, Why? doth not the son bear the iniquity of the father? When the son hath done that which is lawful and right, and hath kept all my statutes, and hath done them, he shall surely live.

²⁰ The soul that sinneth, it shall die. The son shall not bear the iniquity of the father, neither shall the father bear the iniquity of the son: the righteousness of the righteous shall be upon him, and the wickedness of the wicked shall be upon him.

²¹ But if the wicked will turn from all his sins that he hath committed, and keep all my statutes, and do that which is lawful and right, he shall surely live, he shall not die.

²² All his transgressions that he hath committed, they shall not be mentioned unto him: in his righteousness that he hath done he shall live.

²³ Have I any pleasure at all that the wicked should die? saith the Lord GOD: and not that he should return from his ways, and live?

²⁴ But when the righteous turneth away from his righteousness, and committeth iniquity, and doeth according to all the abominations that the wicked man doeth, shall he live? All his righteousness that he hath done shall not be mentioned: in his trespass that he hath trespassed, and in his sin that he hath sinned, in them shall he die.

²⁵ Yet ye say, The way of the Lord is not equal. Hear now, O house of Israel; Is not my way equal? are not your ways unequal?

²⁶ When a righteous man turneth away from his righteousness, and committeth iniquity, and dieth in them; for his iniquity that he hath done shall he die.

27 Again, when the wicked man turneth away from his wickedness that he hath committed, and doeth that which is lawful and right, he shall save his soul alive.

28 Because he considereth, and turneth away from all his transgressions that he hath committed, he shall surely live, he shall not die.

29 Yet saith the house of Israel, The way of the Lord is not equal. O house of Israel, are not my ways equal? are not your ways unequal?

30 Therefore I will judge you, O house of Israel, every one according to his ways, saith the Lord GOD. Repent, and turn yourselves from all your transgressions; so iniquity shall not be your ruin.

31 Cast away from you all your transgressions, whereby ye have transgressed; and make you a new heart and a new spirit: for why will ye die, O house of Israel?

32 For I have no pleasure in the death of him that dieth, saith the Lord GOD: wherefore turn yourselves, and live ye.

Matthew 7:21-23

21 Not every one that saith unto me, Lord, Lord, shall enter into the kingdom of heaven; but he that doeth the will of my Father which is in heaven.

22 Many will say to me in that day, Lord, Lord, have we not prophesied in thy name? and in thy name have cast out devils? and in thy name done many wonderful works?

23 And then will I profess unto them, I never knew you: depart from me, ye that work iniquity.

Matthew 24:11-12

11 And many false prophets shall rise, and shall deceive many.

12 And because iniquity shall abound, the love of many shall wax cold.

Luke 8:11-14

11 Now the parable is this: The seed is the Word of God.

12 Those by the way side are they that hear; then cometh the devil, and taketh away the word out of their hearts, lest they should believe and be saved.

13 They on the rock are they, which, when they hear, receive the word with joy; and these have no root, which for a while believe, and in time of temptation fall away.

14 And that which fell among thorns are they, which, when they have heard, go forth, and are choked with cares and riches and pleasures of this life, and bring no fruit to perfection.

Luke 9:62

And Jesus said unto him, No man, having put his hand to the plough, and looking back, is fit for the kingdom of God.

Luke 11:24-26

24 When the unclean spirit is gone out of a man, he walketh through dry places, seeking rest; and finding none, he

saith, I will return unto my house whence I came out.
²⁵ And when he cometh, he findeth it swept and garnished.
²⁶ Then goeth he, and taketh to him seven other spirits more wicked than himself; and they enter in, and dwell there: and the last state of that man is worse than the first.

Galatians 4:9

But now, after that ye have known God, or rather are known of God, how turn ye again to the weak and beggarly elements, whereunto ye desire again to be in bondage?

1 Timothy 4:1-2

¹ Now the Spirit speaketh expressly, that in the latter times some shall depart from the faith, giving heed to seducing spirits, and doctrines of devils;
² Speaking lies in hypocrisy; having their conscience seared with a hot iron;

James 5:19-20

¹⁹ Brethren, if any of you do err from the truth, and one convert him;
²⁰ Let him know, that he which converteth the sinner from the error of his way shall save a soul from death, and shall hide a multitude of sins.

2 Peter 2:14-15

¹⁴ Having eyes full of adultery, and that cannot cease from sin; beguiling unstable souls: an heart they have exercised with covetous practices; cursed children:

¹⁵ Which have forsaken the right way, and are gone astray, following the way of Balaam the son of Bosor, who loved the wages of unrighteousness;

2 Peter 2:20-22

²⁰ For if after they have escaped the pollutions of the world through the knowledge of the Lord and Saviour Jesus Christ, they are again entangled therein, and overcome, the latter end is worse with them than the beginning.

²¹ For it had been better for them not to have known the way of righteousness, than, after they have known it, to turn from the holy commandment delivered unto them.

²² But it is happened unto them according to the true proverb, The dog is turned to his own vomit again; and the sow that was washed to her wallowing in the mire.

These are some of the scriptures which teach that, yes, **a man can and many do throw away their salvation**. As John says, "*Look to yourselves, beware, take heed that no man rob you of that which God has wrought in you.*"

In Verse 9, John speaks of those who transgress the Word of God, those who have heard the pure Word of God, then given themselves, through repentance, to the Lord Jesus Christ, and become saved through the shed blood. However, because of something that has happened in their lives, they walk away from God and the doctrine of the cross and go back into the world. As John puts it: "*Whosoever transgresseth, and abideth not in the doctrine of Christ, hath not God.*" You can't say it much plainer than that.

You can walk away from the truth and lose your salvation. It would be great if the doctrine of eternal security was true, but it isn't. Just as Judas walked away from Jesus, many today walk away from Jesus and the truth of God's Word. John is so concerned about the saints being led astray that he encourages them to not let anyone into their homes that believes a different doctrine. Then, just as now, there are those who have a form of godliness but deny the power thereof, and **scripture tells us to turn away from them**.

2 Timothy 3:5

> *Having a form of godliness, but denying the power thereof: from such turn away.*

John even goes further and tells us that the saints were not to wish them God speed; this was a type of blessing. **We are not in any way to bless the progress of evil.** To bid these people God speed was to make themselves a partaker of any evil that was done.

2 John 1:12-13

> *[12] Having many things to write unto you, I would not write with paper and ink: but I trust to come unto you, and speak face to face, that our joy may be full.*
> *[13] The children of thy elect sister greet thee. Amen.*

These two verses need no explanation; they are simply John telling the church (the elect lady) that his desire is to come to them and speak face to face. It's hard to put into words what you truly want to say when writing a letter. Speaking face to face, you can discuss problems and ideas, which cannot be done in a letter. However, writing was their only way to communicate other than face to face. They could not just pick up a phone and talk or text one another as we do today.

John closed by saying, *"the children of thy elect sister greet thee."* In our words, he was saying the members of our local church send their greetings to the members of your local church. God be with you and protect you in our Lord's name. May the peace of God be with you. Amen.

2nd John Review Questions

1. One of the devil's main targets is

_____

_____

2. Who is the elect lady?

_____

_____

_____

3. What has set us free from sin and bondage?

_____

_____

4. It is impossible to keep the commandments without a true

_____

_____

5. Where do many of these deceivers come from?

_____

_____

6. The denial of the incarnation is common today among

_____

_____

7. Can we learn anything from the bad things that happens to

us? _____ Yes or _____ No

8. What did John stress about visitors?

_____

_____

_____

9. Do you believe a person can backslide and lose their salva-

tion? _____ Yes or _____ No

10. Believers were not to open their homes to people who were

of a different

_____

_____

3rd John

Introduction to 3rd John

This third Epistle of John is written to Gaius who was, it seems, a personal friend of John's. As in the second epistle, John addresses himself as the elder. So, who was Gaius? Upon searching the scriptures, we find that **there are four men named Gaius in the New Testament**. Not much is known about any one of them. In *Everyone in the Bible*, by William P. Barker, on page 110, we find:

1. A man of Corinth lead to the Lord by Paul who was even baptized by Paul. This Gaius was a leader in the Corinthian church and by all accounts very prominent in the community and city. (I Corinthians 1:14 and Romans 16:23)
2. This Gaius was a very close friend and trusted companion of Paul. This Gaius was known as being of Macedonia.
3. This Gaius was a traveling companion of Paul upon one or more of his trips. This Gaius was from the city of Derbe. (Acts 30:4)
4. The fourth Gaius was the personal friend of John's and showed John hospitality upon occasion. John calls this Gaius his beloved friend.

John commends Gaius for his Christian charity and brotherly love to the saints of God. John also addresses a problem in the local church and is determined that when he comes to visit, he would straighten out everything. When there's confusion in the church, the will of God cannot have its perfect way. When people get out of God's will and into their own will, then the door is opened to Satan, all manner of strife develops and the church is soon ripped apart.

3rd John

3 John 1:1-4

¹ The elder unto the wellbeloved Gaius, whom I love in the truth.
² Beloved, I wish above all things that thou mayest prosper and be in health, even as thy soul prospereth.
³ For I rejoiced greatly, when the brethren came and testified of the truth that is in thee, even as thou walkest in the truth.
⁴ I have no greater joy than to hear that my children walk in truth.

There are today, as in the days of John, battles being fought. The battle for truth rages across the land and in our churches. Our homes as well as our churches are a battleground, where **Satan wages war for the souls of our families and Christian brothers and sisters**. As we look at history, we find that things have not changed much in the spiritual realm. It's still a war of good versus evil.

John writes this letter to Gaius. John addresses himself as the elder to his good and trusted brother in Christ. John loved the brotherhood or fellowship of the saints. He was also quick to give praise where praise was due. As we look at John and how he conducted himself, we should take a lesson. **There's too much criticism in the church and not enough encouragement**, not enough acknowledgement of a job well done. We should look for something good to say every day to those who are around us.

When I speak of too much criticism, I'm not talking about Christians being too hard on sin. Sin is sin, and sin will send the soul to hell. We must take a stand against sin in every shape, form and fashion. What I'm speaking of is that we need to encourage one another, to **lift one another up for their good service in the Lord**.

John saw Gaius as a soldier of the cross of Christ, a lover of the truth of God's Word. In Verse 2, John tells Gaius that his wish or prayer for him was that God would prosper him and give him good health. He also asks God to prosper Gaius' soul, that Gaius might be used of God. In the Old Testament, a person's spiritual prosperity could be gauged by their material prosperity. The closer you walked with God spiritually, the more you were blessed materially. However, in the New Testament, there's a change. In the Old Testament, God spelled out the rules by which the people were to live, and if they obeyed the law, God promised them that He would bless them and make them a great nation.

In the Old Testament, God had only one people, the Jews, but **under grace, the church is made up of not one nation of people, but many people from all nations**. Things have changed. This doesn't mean that the Jews aren't God's people; they are. However, under grace, salvation is given to whosoever will. It's still God's will that we prosper and be in good health, even as our soul prospers. The change is that if we live for God and walk in His footsteps, we're not promised that He'll make us a great nation. We'll be blessed, and we will prosper in God, but under grace, we are a very diverse people.

We're not looking to become a nation, for **the kingdom that we seek is not an earthly kingdom but a heavenly one**. As we look around, we see all kinds of things preached that aren't true. Preachers will take scriptures out of context and build a doctrine. I believe in God's people prospering, but I don't believe in the prosperity preaching that's going on today. If you want to prosper, **live for God, give your life to His service, and I can assure you that you'll be blessed**. If you're sick, God does heal. If we will pray in faith believing, this is God's Word. John's desire was for Gaius to be blessed and to be in good health. The Bible doesn't tell us about Gaius' life. We don't know if he was rich or poor, in good health or sickly. The scriptures don't say. All that we're sure about is that John knew Gaius. I believe that God will give us no more than He can trust us with; some people can't be trusted with very much, or it goes to their head; in other words, they lose all self-control.

In Verse 3, John expresses his joy of hearing a good report of Gaius. As John states that, there were those who came to him from Gaius. The scripture gives no details as to who these visitors might be. Nevertheless, they told of Gaius and his stand for the truth that is in Christ Jesus.

As we look at this scripture, we can only assume that Gaius was a man of good report and well-liked by his brethren. He was an example of Christian love and kindness. This type of example is the kind of witness that we, as Christians, need to be showing forth to the world. **We need to let the world know what we believe and live what we believe before the world.** Too many times we see people who talk good, but their lives don't match up with what they say and what they believe. This is one reason why Christians have such a bad report. We must live what we believe.

In Verse 4, John speaks of his great joy again because of this good report. We don't know if John founded this local church, but he thought of its members as his spiritual children. In addition, to hear that they held fast to the truth of the gospel was joy unmeasurable. We have this same feeling in the ministry. **Pastors, after a short while at a church, begin to look upon their members as their spiritual children.** If for some reason they don't, then something's wrong. There are different callings, and being a pastor of God's flock is a special calling. A pastor isn't like an evangelist. Yes, both are preachers, but **to be a pastor is to stay with the flock,** care for the flock, keep them from harm, laugh with them and yes, even cry with them, loving them as Christ loves them. It's a rewarding life, but it's also a life of sacrifice. John had a pastor's heart.

3 John 1:5-8

⁵ Beloved, thou doest faithfully whatsoever thou doest to the brethren, and to strangers;
⁶ Which have borne witness of thy charity before the church: whom if thou bring forward on their journey after a godly sort, thou shalt do well:
⁷ Because that for his name's sake they went forth, taking nothing of the Gentiles.
⁸ We therefore ought to receive such, that we might be fellowhelpers to the truth.

In Verse 5, we again look at what was expected of the Christian community. When travelers came to their town, and this means other Christians, it was expected of them to open their homes to these travelers. Sometimes they could be ministers, or teachers, or common people traveling. This is why John warned them to be sure of their doctrine, and if it wasn't the same as theirs, not to open up to them their homes.

In that day, it was customary for the travelers to carry letters of recommendation to the local church or to members of the local assembly. **We need to remember how careful Christians had to be with their hospitality and in opening their homes to strangers.** This time period was a time of open persecution of the Christian church and of the Christian followers. As of now, we have never seen times of open persecution of Christians in America, but as Jesus tarries, we may see such days here. Our land is blessed because we've been a Christian nation, but that day is swiftly passing away. **If the people of this country don't turn again to God, we may very well be doomed.** There is still hope if we will raise our voices in prayer calling upon the God of heaven.

2 Chronicles 7:14-15

14 If my people, which are called by my name, shall humble themselves, and pray, and seek my face, and turn from their wicked ways; then will I hear from heaven, and will forgive their sin, and will heal their land.
15 Now mine eyes shall be open, and mine ears attent unto the prayer that is made in this place.

Prayer changes things; prayer can change the mind of God or delay things that are to come. It's time that we do what needs doing; don't wait for someone else to do it. **Get yourself up and work for the Lord and his kingdom.**

In Verse 6, John is writing about the report that he received, about the events that took place as these travelers returned to John. They told of Gaius, his hospitality and his love of God; about his charity, his helpfulness and ministering to their needs; and how when they left, he helped them on their way. Perhaps he gave them food and money for their journey.

It's hard for a church to extend charity when its members won't tithe and give in offerings. Tithing is a principal set forth in the Old Testament and brought forward in the New Testament. **For a church body to function, all its membership must tithe and give in offerings.** When we do so, then there's money to pay the bills, to give to an evangelist or to support missions work. The church should be able to support its pastor and his family. There are people who make a good wage, and they expect the pastor and his family to live on a portion of that amount. But he's still expected to attend to his flock, be at their beck and call, attend all church meetings and conferences and dress himself and his family to meet everyone's standards. He's to open his home to guest speakers and do everything else that's needed. We need to put ourselves in his shoes.

Verse 7 talks about those who worked for God. The custom was to go, relying on the charity of the churches where they went for housing, food and money. However, they were not to beg charity of the unsaved. If charity was offered, they could accept it, but **they were not to beg for charity from the unchurched**. They were to depend on God to supply their need according to His riches in glory.

Verse 8 goes on to tell us that we are to receive Christian workers and to help in whatever way we can to further the work of the gospel. **A minister, a missionary, or whoever gives their full time to the work of God needs to be supported by the**

body, that God may be glorified. It was and is a shame for a full-time minister to be in want.

3 John 1:9-11

⁹ I wrote unto the church: but Diotrephes, who loveth to
have the preeminence among them, receiveth us not.
¹⁰ Wherefore, if I come, I will remember his deeds which
he doeth, prating against us with malicious words: and not
content therewith, neither doth he himself receive the
brethren, and forbiddeth them that would, and casteth
them out of the church.
¹¹ Beloved, follow not that which is evil, but that which is
good. He that doeth good is of God: but he that doeth evil
hath not seen God.

As we look at these scriptures, it seems that nothing has changed. Some pastors obey the gospel and are the servants to their churches. Then **there are those pastors who have become dictators of their churches.** Everything in their churches must revolve around them. They are the high lord and master of their churches and control everything.

Let me quote from *The Wiersbe Bible Commentary:* "Our Lord's disciples often argued over which of them would be the greatest in the kingdom (Matt. 18:1). Jesus had to remind them that their model for ministry was not the Roman official who lorded it over people, but the Saviour Himself who came as a humble servant (Phil. 2:1). During my many years of ministry. I have seen the model for ministry change, and the church is suffering because of it. It appears that the successful minister today is more like a Madison Avenue Tycoon than a submissive servant.

In his hand he holds a wireless telephone, not a towel; in his heart is selfish ambition, not a love for souls and for God's sheep.

"Diotrephes was motivated by pride. Instead of giving the preeminence to Jesus Christ (Col. 1:18) he claimed it for himself. He had the final say-so about everything in the church, and his decisions were determined by one thing, what will this do for Diotrephes? He was most unlike John the Baptist who said, 'He [Jesus Christ] must increase, but I must decrease' (John 3:30)."

Whenever and wherever a church has a dictator in power in the church, there will most certainly be problems. Anyone who desires the freedom of the spirit, the divine moving of God, cannot and will not stay, because **if they stay, they will spiritually die**.

Now in Verse 9, as we look at what John has to say, John is telling Gaius that he wrote to the church. Nevertheless, Diotrephes, who loves to be in control and takes the authority from everyone else, would not receive the letter that John sent. From outward appearance, Diotrephes didn't want to have anything to do with John and John's apostolic authority. Nor did he want any ministers sent by John to preach or teach in the church. Was Diotrephes the pastor? We don't know. Was he the head deacon? Again, we don't know, but he took upon himself all the authority that he could, to the point that **he controlled the church and decided who would do what; whom the church would receive and whom they would reject**.

In Verse 10, John goes on to say that he, if he comes to the church, won't forget what Diotrephes has done, and John determines to set things right. John denounces Diotrephes' attitude and conduct; his prating (to talk excessively and pointlessly; babble) about John and God's servants of truth. **Diotrephes even went so far as to refuse the brethren hospitality and ordered everyone**

in the church to refuse them, also. If they disobeyed him and gave hospitality to these men sent by John, Diotrephes would cast them out of the church body. The shame of it all is that **even to-day there are men and women who follow in the footsteps of Diotrephes**. Yes, we have those today who would be a dictator over God's servants.

In Verse 11, John stresses that **the servant of God is to follow the goodness of God, and they are to reject the very appearance of evil**. The man or woman who follows evil is traveling down a road to a devil's hell. John doesn't ever tell us what he did about Diotrephes taking control of the local church. I would like to think he went and put Diotrephes in his rightful place, but we don't know. The one thing we are sure of is that the spirit that entered into Diotrephes is very much in action today in our churches. **The Lord should be in control, and pastors should be following what God has laid out for us to do.** Following God's plan is the only thing that really works.

3 John 1:12

Demetrius hath good report of all men, and of the truth it-self: yea, and we also bear record; and ye know that our record is true.

We've read about the attitude of Diotrephes and his evil doings. So now, let's look at another man, Demetrius. Demetrius was, according to John, a very good man; a man of good report by all who knew him and his life. He loved the Lord, walked in the truth of God's Word and loved the brethren. As we can gather, **John was sending Demetrius to Gaius, to stand with Gaius**. Diotrephes had overreached himself by destroying John's letter.

Now John sent another letter by the hand of Demetrius, a trusted brother in the Lord. This letter Gaius would get, along with a man to support him. **The devil did not destroy this letter, because it has become part of the Bible, and we are reading it now.** God is not to be played with; if we try, we only dig ourselves into a deep pit, which leads to hell.

3 John 1:13-14

13 I had many things to write, but I will not with ink and pen write unto thee:
14 But I trust I shall shortly see thee, and we shall speak face to face. Peace be to thee. Our friends salute thee. Greet the friends by name.

Verse 13 explains itself; there were many things that John wanted to say to Gaius, but he didn't want to write them all down. He settled for just a short note. His desire was the same to Gaius as it was to the "elect lady," that he should be able to come and speak of the many things he desired to discuss face to face. Letters are good, but setting down together one on one can clear the air of many things. **John was very old, but he had a pastor's heart**; he cared for God's people very much and loved them as Christ loved them.

John, in Verse 14, tells Gaius of his plan visit with him and the local church in the near future. What he was doing was **warning them of what was going to happen in the very near future**. It was also a warning to Diotrephes that John was coming, and he had many things to discuss with the local assembly. One was how could they let themselves be bossed around by Diotrephes, who had become a tyrant? He was out of the will of

God, assuming authority that should not be his; he had bullied the saints, even to ordering them not to give hospitality to the saints that traveled by. Moreover, if he wasn't obeyed, he would cast the disobedient out of the church. He sounds like many of today's so-called preachers. There are pastors today who don't want their people to visit other churches' revivals, homecomings, special events and such. Why are they afraid, because their people might not return? **If a pastor cares for his flock, preaches and teaches the Word, and feeds them spiritually, he needn't worry about losing his people.** In closing, I leave you this warning: guard yourselves, take no one at face value, study the scriptures, and walk in the truth of God. Hold to the doctrine that "was once delivered" to the saints (the whole Bible) and pray, pray, pray.

3rd John Review Questions

1. 3 John was written to whom?

_____

2. How does John address himself?

_____

3. There is too much criticism in the church and not enough

_____

_____

4. We must take a stand against sin in every

_____

and _____.

5. In the New Testament the church is made up of

_____

_____

6. Pastors look upon their members as

_____

_____

7. To be a pastor is to:

_____

_____

8. Traveling ministers were to go forth, relying on the charity

of the churches but they were not to beg charity of the

_____

9. Some pastors are servants to their church and some pastors

have become

_____

_____

10. Diotrephes ordered that no one was to give hospitality to

John's messengers. If they did what would happen to them?

_____

_____

11. Who was the man who had a very good report told about

him? _____

12. To whom did John send Demetrius?

_____

13. Demetrius carried a letter to Gaius. How can we be sure that the devil did not destroy it?

_____

_____

14. John announces that he is coming to see Gaius and the local church. Whom did this warn?

_____

15. Some pastors do not want their church people to visit other churches. What are they afraid will happen?

_____

_____

Bibliography

There's an overwhelming lack of good spiritual material offered to the public today. There are so many misleading books and reference materials that a person hardly knows what's good, and what's not. I have tried, with help from these authors, to give you a fundamental resource that you can study, all of which is based on the King James Version of the Bible. I would like to give my sincere thanks to the following authors for their reference books and materials without which this Bible study would not have been possible. I've prayed and sought God for what He wanted in this study. I read these authors' material, their thoughts and opinions, and it has opened up a lot of knowledge, which by prayer I have tried to use wisely. Thank you very much.

Brother Wilson

Rev. Matthew Henry
Matthew Henry's Commentary on the Whole Bible

Rev. Albert Barnes
Barnes Notes on the New Testament

Rev. Finis Jennings Dake
The Dake Annotated Reference Bible

Rev. Frank Thompson D.D., P.H.D.
Thompson Chain Reference Bible

Rev. Warren W. Wiersbe
The Wiersbe Bible Commentary

Rev. John R. W. Stott
Tyndale New Testament Commentaries

Adam Clarke
Commentary on the Bible

Jay P. Green Sr.
General Editor and Translator
The Interlinear Bible

Hebrew, Greek, English
James Strong, S.T.D., L.L.D.
Strong's Exhaustive Concordance of the Bible

Joseph S. Exell
The Biblical Illustrator

Rev. David Wilson
A Study on the Holy Ghost

Test Your Knowledge Answers

1st John

Introduction & Chapter One (page 37)

1. A battle ground of good and evil
2. a. Ebionites
   b. Docetists
   c. Cerinthians
3. a. Peter
   b. James
   c. John
4. Word
5. Because of false teaching coming into the church.
6. Counterfeit
7. The life
8. Children of the devil
9. He needs fellowship
10. Momentary
11. Thy salvation
12. Abolition of religion
13. Light
14. Builder and maker is God
15. By staying in the light as He is in the light
16. Yes
17. No, a lie is a lie
18. Yes
19. Yes
20. Through Jesus

Chapter Two (page 99)

1. Anything that comes between you and God
2. Jesus Christ
3. Advocate with the Father
4. They don't read or study their Bible
5. Yes
6. By the blood of the Lamb and the word of our testimony
7. By keeping His commandments
8. No
9. They are:
   a. Love
   b. Life
   c. Light
10. Faith
11. The sinner
12. We, the people whose names are written in the Book of Life
13. Wounds
14. They are:
   a. The father or elder
   b. The young men
   c. The children
15. Work force of the church
16. They are old
17. **1 John 2:15** *Love not the world, neither the things that are in the world. If any man love the world, the love of the Father is not in him.*

18. They are:
    a. The lust of the flesh
    b. The lust of the eyes
    c. The pride of life
19. **Hebrews 11:10** . . . *a city which hath foundations, whose builder and maker is God.*
20. The here and now
21. An unction
22. A special God-given anointing
23. Everyone who denies that Jesus is the Son of God
24. **Psalm 51:12** . . . *the joy of thy salvation;* . . .
25. Eternal Life
26. To draw the saints away from God
27. No
28. Sowers of seed
29. The anointing
30. Lord's return for his church
31. Pay the consequences

Chapter 3 (page 145)

1. The son-ship of God
2. Sons and daughters of God
3. They are:
    a. By birth
    b. By adoption
    c. By marriage
4. The saved church of God
5. Yes

6. When Jesus came and fulfilled the law
7. Yes, they are
8. What is sin?
9. To serve him
10. Will
11. Yes
12. Pride
13. Saved
14. The spirit man
15. Binds us together
16. It is a life of service to God and to his people, the church
17. Abel
18. Deeds
19. Noah
20. Every knee shall bow and every tongue shall confess that Jesus is Lord

Chapter 4 (page 177)

1. a. To believe not every spirit.
   b. To try the spirits to see if they are of God.
2. Nine
3. a. The group of Revelation
   b. The group of Power
   c. The group of Utterance
4. The truth about a person spiritually
5. He that is in the world
6. a. The Word of God abides in you
   b. The seed of God abides in you
   c. God, Himself, abides in you

7. Yes
8. Power of God
9. Saints
10. They put on a good show
11. Because their sins have already been forgiven and they have already been judged at the judgment seat of Christ.
12. Fear
13. What language can tell
14. Liar
15. Agent
16. We do
17. Faith
18. Preach the pure Word of God.
19. Confident

Chapter 5 (page 213)

1. The last three verses of Chapter 4.
2. If we love God then we will keep His commandments
3. They are:
    a. Faith
    b. Hope
    c. Confidence in the Lord
4. Jesus
5. They are:
    a. Act like Christ acted
    b. Do as Christ did
    c. Love as Christ loved
6. Gives us the victory

7. Comforter
8. Dangerous thing
9. Our days of grace
10. Because it took that long for Noah to build the Ark and make all the preparations before the rain began to fall.
11. Not one drop of blood is used
12. They are:
    a. The Father
    b. The Word
    c. Holy Ghost
13. They are:
    a. The spirit
    b. The water
    c. The blood
14. Evolution is a theory without any facts supporting it.
15. They will be because they will give up without a fight.
16. Confidence
17. They are:
    a. We have not because we ask not
    b. Or because we ask amiss
18. The only place to find permanent peace is in God.
19. The blasphemy of, or sin against, the Holy Ghost
20. The only way to go to heaven is through Jesus Christ. We must accept Him as our personal Savior.

2nd John

(page 239)

1. The home, especially the Christian homes
2. It is believed that it was one of the local churches

3. The truth
4. Love for God
5. Out of the church
6. Liberal theologians
7. Yes
8. No one was to be taken at face value
9. Answer this how you personally believe
10. Doctrine

3rd John

(page 257)

1. Gaius
2. The elder
3. Encouragement and acknowledgement of jobs well done
4. Shape, form and fashion
5. Many people from all nations
6. Their spiritual children
7. Stay with the flock, care for the flock, keep them from harm, laugh with them, and yes, even cry with them, love them as Christ loves them.
8. Unsaved
9. Dictators
10. Be cast out of the church
11. Demetrius
12. Gaius
13. Because it is now the book we know as 3rd John.
14. Diotrephes
15. They are afraid that their church members will leave their church.

— Notes —

— Notes —

— Notes —

Coming Fall 2017!

Look for Rev. Wilson's upcoming study on ***The Revelation of Jesus Christ*** through **Paradise Gospel Press** and **Amazon**. Enjoy the following excerpt from the book:

Chapter 1

Revelation 1:1

The Revelation of Jesus Christ, which God gave unto him, to shew unto his servants things which must shortly come to pass; and he sent and signified it by his angel unto his servant John:

The book of Revelation is a book that contains the revelation of Jesus Christ, which God gave to him for one specific purpose. What is that? To show unto his servant John things *"which must shortly come to pass."* **Revelation, despite what many people believe or say, is not the revelation of John.** The Word tells us point blank that the book of Revelation is the revelation of Jesus Christ. John was only the vessel that Jesus used to write the warning to the churches and to the saints of what the future holds for the world. To those who disbelieve Revelation, and there are many, I turn your attention to 2 Timothy 3:16-17. *"All scripture is given by inspiration of God, and is profitable for doctrine, for re-*

Note: In this study, all scripture is quoted from the *King James Version* unless otherwise stated. All scriptures are italicized.

proof, for correction, for instruction in righteousness: That the man of God may be perfect, thoroughly furnished unto all good works." Many people in our churches today pick and choose what scriptures they want to believe. But **the Word plainly states that all scripture is given by the inspiration of God**. There can be no picking and choosing; we must accept the whole Word of God. Another scripture to look at is 2 Timothy 4:1-2. *"I charge thee therefore before God, and the Lord Jesus Christ, who shall judge the quick and the dead at his appearing and his kingdom; Preach the word; be instant in season, out of season; reprove, rebuke, exhort with all long-suffering and doctrine."* Sadly to say, this shows us a picture of our modern-day churches, **turning from scripture and changing scripture to say what they want it to say**. They teach that under grace no one will miss heaven, that Jesus died for the whole world. Sin and sinners are welcomed into their churches. They ordain homosexuals as priest and pastors, something God's Word strictly forbids and condemns. I touch on these subjects to get them out of the way, so that we can keep our minds on Revelation. It's Jesus' Revelation, which God, His Father, gave to Him. Jesus then sent and signified it, by his angel, unto His servant John. Nowhere is John called the revelator.

Revelation 1:2

² Who bare record of the word of God, and of the testimony of Jesus Christ, and of all things that he saw.

The testimony of John is that he remained true to his calling in Christ Jesus. The scripture states of John, *"Who bare record of the word of God, and of the testimony of Jesus Christ, and of all things that he saw."* This Revelation tells us of the things that will be taking place on the earth as well as things taking place in heaven **before, during and after the rapture of the saints or the church**.

Revelation 1:3

³ Blessed is he that readeth, and they that hear the words of this prophecy, and keep those things which are written therein: for the time is at hand.

Blessed are they – who? The people who read and hear the words of this prophecy and keep those things – what things? The things that are written in this book, because the time is at hand – what time is at hand? The soon return of our Lord Jesus Christ to take us, the saints, home to glory. **This book is a warning to the child of God and to the churches, to get as many saved as possible before Jesus comes back.** As we look at those around us who claim to be saved, we find that many of them had rather believe a lie than the truth. But it is only the truth that will set us free.

Revelation 1:4-8

⁴ John to the seven churches which are in Asia: Grace be unto you, and peace, from him which is, and which was, and which is to come; and from the seven Spirits which are before his throne;
⁵ And from Jesus Christ, who is the faithful witness, and the first begotten of the dead, and the prince of the kings of the earth. Unto him that loved us, and washed us from our sins in his own blood,

⁶ And hath made us kings and priests unto God and his Father; to him be glory and dominion for ever and ever. Amen.

⁷ Behold, he cometh with clouds; and every eye shall see him, and they also which pierced him: and all kindreds of the earth shall wail because of him. Even so, Amen.

⁸ I am Alpha and Omega, the beginning and the ending, saith the Lord, which is, and which was, and which is to come, the Almighty.

John begins to write to the seven churches which are in Asia. He begins with a greeting from our Lord and the seven Spirits which are before the throne. **John must have been well known to the churches**, because he simply states, *"John to the seven churches."* The seven Spirits denote the seven-fold ministry of the Holy Ghost. *"There is one Holy Ghost, but as the one candle holder has seven branches for seven candles, the Holy Ghost as the executive person of the Holy Trinity has seven ministry names, namely the Spirit of Adoption, the Spirit of Truth, the Spirit of Supplication, the Spirit of Glory, the Spirit of Holiness, the Spirit of Life, and the Spirit of Wisdom."* (Which denotes a seven-fold ministry with the emphasis being placed on the completeness of the Holy Ghost's ministry.) But **Jesus is the theme of Revelation**. *"He is given three titles and they are: 'Faithful Witness, First Begotten of the Dead and Ruler of the King of the Earth.'"* Then we see what Jesus has done for the church. Unto Him that loved us and washed us from our sins in His own blood. We are made kings and priests unto God. Be glory forever and ever.

Jesus is coming back. **The scripture says that He is coming** with clouds, every eye shall see him, and all the people of the earth shall wail. **Jesus tells us who He is**: the Alpha and Omega, the beginning and the end, the Almighty.

Revelation 1:9-10

⁹ I John, who also am your brother, and companion in tribulation, and in the kingdom and patience of Jesus Christ, was in the isle that is called Patmos, for the word of God, and for the testimony of Jesus Christ.
¹⁰ I was in the Spirit on the Lord's day, and heard behind me a great voice, as of a trumpet,

In *Prevision of History*, by Rev. Elizabeth Williams, D. D., **John identifies himself without titles of honor or rank**; he simply calls himself brother and companion in tribulation, waiting in Christ Jesus. He names the place where he was the isle called Patmos, a small, barren island off the west coast of Asia Minor. He states that he is there for the Word of God and the testimony of Jesus Christ. According to Eusebius, an early church historian, John was banished or exiled to Patmos by the Roman Emperor Domitian in the year A.D. 95.

John further tells us that **he was in the spirit on the Lord's Day**. It simply should be accepted that John means that it was the first day of the week, what we call Sunday, the day of our Lord's resurrection.

Acts 20:7

⁷ And upon the first day of the week, when the disciples came together to break bread, Paul preached unto them, ready to depart on the morrow; and continued his speech until midnight.

1 Corinthians 16:2

² Upon the first day of the week let every one of you lay by him in store, as God hath prospered him, that there be no gatherings when I come.

John 20:19-20

¹⁹ Then the same day at evening, being the first day of the week, when the doors were shut where the disciples were assembled for fear of the Jews, came Jesus and stood in the midst, and saith unto them, Peace be unto you.
²⁰ And when he had so said, he shewed unto them his hands and his side. Then were the disciples glad, when they saw the Lord.

Revelation 1:11-20

¹¹ Saying, I am Alpha and Omega, the first and the last: and, What thou seest, write in a book, and send it unto the seven churches which are in Asia; unto Ephesus, and unto Smyrna, and unto Pergamos, and unto Thyatira, and unto Sardis, and unto Philadelphia, and unto Laodicea.
¹² And I turned to see the voice that spake with me. And being turned, I saw seven golden candlesticks;
¹³ And in the midst of the seven candlesticks one like unto the Son of man, clothed with a garment down to the foot, and girt about the paps with a golden girdle.
¹⁴ His head and his hairs were white like wool, as white as snow; and his eyes were as a flame of fire;
¹⁵ And his feet like unto fine brass, as if they burned in a

furnace; and his voice as the sound of many waters.
16 And he had in his right hand seven stars: and out of his mouth went a sharp twoedged sword: and his countenance was as the sun shineth in his strength.
17 And when I saw him, I fell at his feet as dead. And he laid his right hand upon me, saying unto me, Fear not; I am the first and the last:
18 I am he that liveth, and was dead; and, behold, I am alive for evermore, Amen; and have the keys of hell and of death.
19 Write the things which thou hast seen, and the things which are, and the things which shall be hereafter;
20 The mystery of the seven stars which thou sawest in my right hand, and the seven golden candlesticks. The seven stars are the angels of the seven churches: and the seven candlesticks which thou sawest are the seven churches.

The great voice that John heard in Verse 10 is identified in Verse 11 of this chapter. Jesus tells us who He is by saying, "*I am Alpha and Omega, the first and the last.*" Then John is instructed that everything he is shown, he is to write in a book. Once it is written, **John is to send a copy to each of the seven churches which are in Asia**. Again, these seven churches are: Ephesus, Smyrna, Pergamos, Thyatira, Sardis, Philadelphia and Laodicea. In Verse 12, John turned to see the voice that spoke to him. John states that **he saw seven golden candlesticks, and in the midst of these candlesticks, John saw one like unto the Son of Man**, clothed with a garment down to His feet, having on a golden girdle. His head and His hair are white like wool, as white as snow. **In the Word of God, white denotes purity, without spot or stain, undefiled. It also speaks of wisdom and maturity, denot-**

ing the wisdom of the ages.

His eyes are like as a flame of fire. Here we see a simile describing the all-seeing, all-penetrating, all-knowing power of Jesus Christ. **This flame can burn out the dross in a life and at the same time warm the heart of the believer.** His feet are compared to fine brass, as if they burned in a furnace. **This symbolizes the power that enables Jesus to tread upon the enemy of our souls; nothing can bar or block His path.** His voice is as the sound of many waters. Have you ever stood next to a large waterfall? The sound is deafening. **This is like Jesus as He shows forth His power and glory. He commands and is obeyed.** In His right hand, He holds seven stars. Out of His mouth goes a sharp, two-edged sword. **The sword can be said to be the Word of God, and as Jesus speaks, His word is final.** As John sees this, he is overwhelmed and falls as one dead before the Lord.

The Lord reaches down, lays His right hand on John and tells him not to be afraid or fearful. Jesus reassures John of who He is by saying, *"I am the first and the last. I am he that liveth and was dead; and behold I am alive for evermore."* Jesus is telling John to remember when He walked with him, when He was crucified and when He rose from the dead. **He wants John to remember how they talked and preached God's Word.**

Again, Jesus tells John to write the things which he has seen, and the things that are and that are coming, for these things are warnings to the world and to His church to prepare for His return. The church is going to face trials and tribulations. For a long time, the church has been at ease, but things are changing. **Jesus tells us to fear not, for He is in control. These things must happen, but we are not to fear, for our trust is in Jesus Christ, our Savior.**

Jesus tells John that the seven stars which he saw in Jesus' right hand are the angels of the seven churches. As we look at this mystery, John wasn't writing to angels from heaven, but to the pastors of the seven churches, **those who were responsible for the preaching of the gospel and keeping the churches in line with God's Word**. The seven golden candlesticks are represented as the seven churches in Asia. We can truly say that these seven churches were the most influential churches of that time. They were larger and more active in the ministry of the gospel than any others.

There's a problem when studying the book of Revelation. Many people look at these scriptures and say they don't understand what they are reading. How do we know what's what? Some have said, "I don't read it because it scares me." The book of Revelation must be studied with much prayer. Some scriptures are written as fact, to be taken just as they are written, and some as symbolism, such as the angels of the churches, who are the pastors. Other scriptures are parenthetical. As a rule, most people want everything laid out for them. However, **when it comes to God's Word, there are times when we must dig out what God wants us to know**. The book of Revelation is a picture of the near future; the coming future of mankind. **We cannot be like many people and hide our heads in the sand. Jesus loves us enough to give us warning. Use it, and let it make you a better person.**

www.ingramcontent.com/pod-product-compliance
Lightning Source LLC
Chambersburg PA
CBHW060254100426
42742CB00011B/1746